Kaiulani:

CROWN PRINCESS OF HAWAII

Also by Nancy Webb and Jean Francis Webb

THE HAWAIIAN ISLANDS: From Monarchy to Democracy

KAIULANI:

CROWN PRINCESS OF HAWAII

BY NANCY WEBB
AND JEAN FRANCIS WEBB

New York · THE VIKING PRESS

This book is dedicated to

LALLY

because we love her

Contents

Mahalo

When a story never before fully told in print must be pieced together, fragment by often forgotten fragment, what single writer or team of writers possibly could reassemble it alone? The very nature of their project presupposes dependence upon the generosity of those having custody of the scattered scraps. Certainly no full portrait of Kaiulani, Crown Princess of Hawaii, could be created, six decades after her death, without such help in ample measure.

The Hawaiians have a word, *mahalo,* which, although frequently translated as "thank you," has (in the way of Hawaiian words) extra and unrenderable overtones of warmth. *Mahalo* also may mean "wonder." And it was with considerable wonder, as well as thanks, that we experienced the various kindnesses and near-miracles which added so much to our knowledge of Kaiulani.

Mahalo, then, to Gertrude Heydtmann (Mrs. Victor E.) Friden, who by sheer chance heard Nancy Webb discussing Kaiulani on a radio program in Oregon, and wrote the station to say that she would make available to us the Ainahau journals of her mother, the little Princess's beloved governess, Miss Gardinier.

Mahalo to our teen-age son Toby, who first called to our attention the portrait used on this book's jacket and discovered on a map in a summer hotel in Maine a sketch of the bark *Kaiulani* which led us, in turn, to Mr. Arthur Sewall of the Bath shipbuilding Sewalls. And *mahalo* to Mr. Sewall, who is the son of the last United States Minister to Hawaii and was christened there on Annexation Day, for allowing us to work for several rewarding days among the private Hawaiian papers in his father's library.

Mahalo to the memory of Isobel Strong Field, stepdaughter of Robert Louis Stevenson, who before her death generously wrote from her sickbed her own recollections of Kaiulani—and of her famous stepfather's friendship with the royal child. *Mahalo*, too, to Mrs. Matilda Papaleaiaina Constable of Honolulu, who entrusted to us family accounts of Kaiulani's association with her grandfather, John Cummins.

Our special thanks to Mr. Geoffrey C. Davies, grandson of Kaiulani's guardian, who put himself to considerable trouble to track down Davies material borrowed by another writer unwilling to return it, and who pled our cause with his aunt, Mrs. Alice Davies Warner, Kaiulani's closest friend during her English school years.

Our warm appreciation to the clerk to the Wellingborough Council, Northamptonshire, England, who answered a plea for information on Great Harrowden Hall by putting us in contact with the Hall's present occupant, William Gordon Gilbey, Esq.; and to Mr. Gilbey for his photographs and wonderfully detailed descriptions and history of this ancient seat of the Lords Vaux, once temporarily a school for young ladies.

Mahalo to Ruth Bancroft Powell of the Kaiulani School, Honolulu, for supplying us with a copy of her own manuscript biography of "Hawaii's Hope," and for unstintingly sharing with us source materials she had assembled.

Mahalo to Kathleen Dickenson Mellen, whose books on the Islands form their finest history, for many helpful suggestions and for her pioneer exploration of the true facts of a garbled period; and to Robert Van Dyke, for sharing the Kaiulani momentos of his private museum of Hawaiiana; and to *kamaaina* writer Emma Lyons Doyle, for Cleghorn data obligingly tracked down for us; and to *Advertiser* columnist and historian Clarisse B. Taylor, for similar generous assistance.

Mahalo to Annis Duff, most patient and creative of editors, for guidance and encouragement and for molding an unwieldy first script into a book. *Mahalo* to Agnes C. Conrad of the Archives of Hawaii and to all her staff (especially Aurora Williams Domingo), who provided us with office space and weeks of research materials and whose suggestions led us to much buried treasure. And to Miss Janet Bell, for making available the library resources of the University of Hawaii. And to Pola (Mrs. Hal) Chase for "digging" in San Francisco.

Thanks in more New England fashion to Miss Jean Glasscock, of Wellesley College, for information as to Kaiulani's visit there; and to Sally Meyer, Class of 1963, for interrupting her own term examinations to search the town newspaper's files for additional details.

Our sincere gratitude to Dr. Alexander Spoehr, who turned us loose among trunkfuls of still unclassified old letters in the Bishop Museum, Honolulu; and to his associates, particularly Margaret Titcomb and Heather Saunders, who helped us search out relevant material; and to Mary Kawena Pukui, the Museum's translator and distinguished Hawaiian scholar, who as a kindness rendered into English for the first time old letters concerning Kaiulani.

Mahalo to Mr. Richard Smart, present owner of Hawaii's fabled Parker Ranch, who rescued for us a series of family letters presenting the full picture of Mana as it was when Kaiulani made her final visit there. And to Honolulu's dean of photographers, Ray Jerome Baker, whose files are a priceless pictorial history of Island yesterdays and royal personages.

Where can such a record of gratitude find its ending? Not without mention of Mrs. Burton Holmes for her careful check of her late husband's material on his Hawaiian experiences. Not without acknowledgment of Eleanor Robson (Mrs. August) Belmont's generously furnished memories of Kaiulani and gracious permission to quote from her book, *The Fabric of Memory* (New York: Farrar, Straus and Cudahy, 1957). Not without thanks to Lucinda Bukeley, for research assistance; to Louise Judd, for finding people who still remember "our" Princess; to Caroline Farrand, for the same kind service half a world from Hawaii; to Juliette

Kimball, for personal reminiscences; to Natalie Webb, for editorial suggestions; to Clarence (Buster) Crabbe for family data; to Maili Yardley; to many, many others.

The list is, apparently, endless. Yet no more so than our wonder at the many doors all these people opened for us; the many lucky chances which brought to light material hitherto unpublished; the many unanticipated discoveries to which our informants have led us. To all of them, and from our hearts—*Mahalo!*

NANCY WEBB
JEAN FRANCIS WEBB

"Sabrina Rock"
South Salem
New York

A Note about Hawaiian Words

Because Hawaiian words so often appear difficult to the eye, a natural tendency develops in the reader to avoid them. It is easier to skip to a following word with a shape which appears more familiar. In this way, a great deal of the special flavor of lilting Island speech can be lost. With the hope of making it possible for readers of this book to enjoy (rather than to escape from) the few Hawaiian words they will encounter, we have attempted this brief and admittedly over-simplified comment on pronunciations.

The Hawaiian tongue was created to be spoken. And, properly spoken, it is one of the most satisfying to the ear of all languages employed by man.

Until the arrival of the first Christian missionaries to the Islands in 1820, however, there was no written Hawaiian. The literature of the people was passed down from generation to generation by chanters with memories so exactingly trained that not a syllable of the old legends and genealogies would be altered through many re-tellings. With the arrival of the missionaries—who wished to print Bibles and hymns for their converts—a written language was developed, based upon the one the New Englanders heard spoken around them.

The written Hawaiian thus brought into being is based upon an alphabet of twelve letters—the vowels A, E, I, O, U, and the consonants H, K, L, M, N, P and W. In addition, and perhaps to be considered an extra consonant, is the *'u'ina,* represented by an inverted comma, which stands for an earlier Polynesian "K" almost lost through elision. The presence of the *'u'ina* in a word can completely alter its sense. *Pau* (pow) means "finished," "done"; but *pa'u* (pah-oo) means "a woman's riding skirt."

In the pronunciation of English words, both vowels and consonants very often are silent; and it is more frequently the consonants which give a word its character. By contrast, in Hawaiian many words contain no consonants at all; and the vowels are of very great importance, all vowels and consonants being carefully sounded. Each syllable of a Hawaiian word ends in a vowel. Two consonants never occur together. A vowel sound is never carried to a consonant following it as part of the same syllable.

In spoken Hawaiian, the accent of a word falls most usually upon the next-to-last syllable. Many words are not accented at all. There are very few inflections in Hawaiian pronunciation. And, in general, each vowel is apt to be sounded as an individual syllable.

The vowels are sounded thus:

> A "ah" as in "farmer"
> E "ay" as in "obey"
> I "ee" as in "police"
> O "oh" as in "cozy"
> U "oo" as in "rude"

The consonants are pronounced as they are in English, with some few exceptions. K and L, pronounced in modern Hawaiian as in English, originally had more the sounds, respectively, of T and R. And the Hawaiian W may be a soft W, as in *Waikiki,* or something approaching a soft V, as in *Ewa* (ev-ah). The *'u'ina* is sounded somewhat like a grunt.

Hawaiian words and proper names to be encountered in this life story of Princess Kaiulani include the following:

Ahuula (ah-hoo-oo-la). A feathered cloak.

Ainahau (ay-na-how). "Place touched by cool breeze," the name of the Cleghorn estate at Waikiki.

Aku (ah-koo). A Hawaiian fish.

Akule (ah-koo-lee). A red Hawaiian fish, the appearance of a school of which was thought to foretell the death of an *alii*.

Alii (ah-lee-ee). A chief or a king; the highest nobility.

Aloha (ah-low-ha). "Love," a word used in Hawaiian greeting and parting.

Aloha Aina (ah-low-ha aye-nah). A patriotic society in Hawaii.

Auaukai (ow-ow-kaye). "To bath in the sea," an earlier name for Ainahau.

Auwe (ah-way). Alas! My goodness!

E (eh). By.

Eleu (el-eh-oo). "Lively," the name of a small Island steamer.

Haawi ke aloha (ha-ah-wee kay ah-low-ha). "To give love," the obligation of the *alii* to their people.

Haku mele (hah-koo meh-leh). "To weave song"; hence, a poet.

Hale Aniani (hah-leh ah-nee-ah-nee). "House of glass," the name of the Honolulu residence of Walter Murray Gibson.

Haole (how-lee). Originally, any foreigner; but coming to mean in particular the Caucasian foreigner.

Hau (how). Breeze; also, the name of an Hawaiian tree.

Hawaii (hah-wah-ee). The archipelago of islands making up the kingdom, territory, and finally state of Hawaii; also, the largest of these islands, locally known as the Big Island.

Heiau (hay-ow). A sacred place, or open-air temple.

Hii (hee-ee). To hold in one's arms, or embrace.

Hilo (hee-low). Chief town on the island of Hawaii.

Holoku (hoh-loh-koo). "Move-stand"; the name given to the garment like an old-fashioned nightgown first made for the Hawaiian women by missionaries, whose sewing machines moved and stopped in the process of creating it.

Honolulu (hoh-noh-loo-loo). The capital city of Hawaii.

Hookupu (hoo-koo-poo). "A contribution"; traditionally, a bearing of gifts to one of the *alii*.

Hui Leahi (hoo-ee lay-ah-hee). A patriotic society in Hawaii.

I (ee). To speak.

Ihe (ee-hay). A war spear.

Ilima (ee-lee-mah). The royal Hawaiian flower, gold-orange in color.

Iolani (ee-o-lah-nee). "Hawk of Heaven," the name of the royal palace in Honolulu.

Ka (kah). The; or, belonging to.

Kaawaloa (kah-ah-wah-lo-ah). "The very harbor," name of Princess Likelike's vacation house on the island of Hawaii.

Kahakukaakoi (kah-hah-koo-ka-ah-koh-ee). Kaiulani's first nurse.

Kahili (kah-hee-lee). A feathered standard, the original Hawaiian equivalent for a flag or banner.

Kahuna (ka-hoo-nah). Properly, an expert in any special field; but corrupted by foreigners in Hawaii to mean witch-doctor.

Kaiulani (kah-ee-oo-lah-nee, but usually elided to kaye-oo-lah-nee). Name of the last Crown Princess of Hawaii.

Kalakaua (kah-lah-cow-ah). Name of the seventh reigning monarch of Hawaii.

Kalani (kah-lah-nee). A gallon.

Kalanianaole (kah-lah-nee-ah-na-o-lee). Prince Jonah Kuhio Kalanianaole was the younger of two nephews and adopted sons of King Kalakaua.

Kalaupapa (kah-lauw-pah-pah). "The flat leaf," name of the leper settlement on the island of Molokai.

Kamaaina (kah-mah-eye-nah). A native born to a place.

Kamani (kah-mah-nee). A Hawaiian tree.

Kamehameha (kah-may-ha-may-ha). The name of each of the first five kings of Hawaii, but particularly of the first king, Kamehameha the Great, whose armies united the Islands under one rule.

Kanaka (kah-nah-kah). A man.

Kanoah (kah-no-ah). Name of a maid serving Princess Kaiulani.

Kapa (kah-pah). A Hawaiian quilt.

Kapena (kah-pay-nah). Name of an official in Kalakaua's government.

Kapili (kah-pee-lee). To join; that which is related to.

Kapiolani (kah-pee-o-lah-nee). Name of King Kalakaua's Queen.

Kapu (kah-poo). Tabu, forbidden.

Kau (cow). A region on the island of Hawaii; also, a kind of wood.

Kaua (kah-oo-ah). To invite to remain.

Kauhane (kah-oo-hah-nee). A member of the House of Nobles during the reign of Queen Liliuokalani.

Kaukau (cow-cow). Food.

Kaumakapili (cow-mah-kah-pee-lee). Name of a native church in old Honolulu.

Kawaiahao (kah-wah-ee-a-hah-o). Name of the foremost native church in Honolulu, known as the Westminster Abbey of Hawaii.

Kawananakoa (kah-wah-nah-nah-ko-ah). Elder of two nephews of his wife adopted by King Kalakaua, and designated his heir after his sister Liliuokalani and his niece Kaiulani.

Ke (kay). The.

Kealakekua (kay-ah-lah-kay-koo-ah). "The pathway of the gods," a bay on the island of Hawaii so named because of its spectacular rainbows like heavenly bridges.

Keelikolani (kay-eh-lee-koh-lah-nee). Second name of Princess Ruth, blood descendant of King Kamehameha I.

Keiki (kay-kee). Child.

Kekaulike (kay-cow-lee-kay). Name of a princess, sister of Queen Kapiolani.

Kinau (kee-now). Name of an inter-island boat.

Kipuupuu (kee-poo-oo-poo-oo). "The squirting joints," name given the driving rains of the Big Island's mountain areas.

"Koa" (koh-ah). Nickname for Prince David Kawananankoa.

Koa (koh-ah). A Hawaiian tree and wood.

Kokua (koh-coo-ah). Help.

Kona (koh-nah). Name of a district on the island of Hawaii.

Kou (koh-oo). Moist; also, yours or mine.

Kuhio (coo-hee-oh). Familiar name for Prince Kalanianaole.

Kukui (coo-coo-ee). A Hawaiian tree.

Kuleana (coo-lay-ah-nah). An ownership; a homestead.

Kuokoa (coo-oh-koh-ah). Standing by oneself; the name of a native newspaper in Hawaii during Kalakaua's time.

Lanai (lah-na-ee, generally elided to lah-nye). One of the chief Hawaiian islands; also, Hawaiian veranda or open-air living room.

Lani (lah-nee). The sky.

Lehua (lay-hoo-ah). A Hawaiian flower.

Lei (lay). A wreath.

Likelike (lee-kay-lee-kay). Name of a Hawaiian Princess, sister to King Kalakaua and mother to Princess Kaiulani.

Liliu (lee-lee-oo). Short form of Liliuokalani.

Liliuokalani (lee-lee-oo-oh-kah-lah-nee). Name of a Hawaiian Princess, elder sister and heir to King Kalakaua; later, the Queen.

Lono (loh-noh). Name of the chief of the Hawaiian gods.

Luau (loo-ow). A feast.

Mahalo (mah-hah-loh). Thanks; also, wonder, amazement.

Maile (my-lee). A perfumed vine, much used in garlands.

Makai (mah-kaye). "Toward the sea," a direction in Hawaii.

Makua (mah-koo-ah). A parent.

Manoa (mah-no-ah). Name of a valley on the island of Oahu.

Maui (mauw-ee). Name of one of the chief Hawaiian islands.

Mauka (mauw-kah). "Toward the mountains," a direction in Hawaii.

Maunawili (mauw-nah-wee-lee). "Twisting mountain," the name of the country home on Oahu of James H. Boyd.

Me (may). With, like.

Mele (meh-lee). A song or poem.

Moi (moh-ee). The King.

Mokolii (moh-koh-lee-ee). Name of an inter-island steamer.

Molokai (moh-loh-kaye). Name of one of the chief Hawaiian islands.

Na (nah). Peaceful.

Nana (nah-nah). For him.

Nei (neh-ee). This one.

No (noh). Of, for.

Nui (noo-ee). Large, great.

Nuuanu (noo-oo-ah-noo). Name of a valley on the island of Oahu.

Oahu (oh-ah-hoo). Name of the most important of the Hawaiian islands, on which the capital city of Honolulu is located.

Olioli (oh-lee-oh-lee). Much happiness.

Oo (oh-oh). A Hawaiian bird, prized for its feathers.

Opehe (oh-pee-hee). A Hawaiian fish.

Pale (pah-leh). An outer garment.

Paniolo (pah-nee-oh-loh). A Hawaiian cowboy.

Pele (peh-lee). Hawaiian goddess of the volcano.

Pikake (pee-kah-kee). The Chinese jasmine in Hawaii, its name a corruption of the English word "peacock"—so called because it was the favorite flower of Kaiulani, identified with her peacocks.

Po (poh). Night.

Poi (poy). A paste of pounded taro, staple of the Hawaiian diet.

Ponoi (poh-noh-ee). "The thing itself"; used to indicate intensification.

Poomaikalani (poo-oo-maye-kah-lah-nee). Name of a Princess, sister to Queen Kapiolani.

Punahou (poo-nah-hoe). "Fresh spring," the name of a famous school in Hawaii.

Ti (tee). A Hawaiian plant.

Ululani (oo-loo-lah-nee). Name of a famous poetess of early Hawaii, the great-great-grandmother of Princess Kaiulani.

Waikiki (waye-kee-kee). Name of a beach suburb of the city of Honolulu.

Waimanalo (waye-mah-nah-loh). The country estate on Oahu of John Cummins; also, the name of a private steamer belonging to Mr. Cummins.

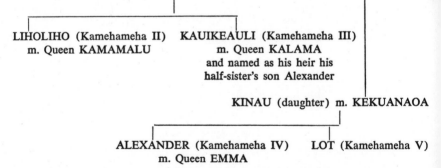

The Royal Succession in Hawaii

Hawaii's throne did not of necessity, as in most other kingdoms, descend from father to eldest son. Instead, each monarch had the privilege of designating his own official successor. As conqueror and unifier of the Islands in 1795, Kamehameha I founded the dynasty bearing his own name.

KAMEHAMEHA I m. Queen KEOPUOLANI and also Queen KAHEIHEIMAILE

LIHOLIHO (Kamehameha II)   KAUIKEAULI (Kamehameha III)
    m. Queen KAMAMALU   m. Queen KALAMA
                              and named as his heir his
                              half-sister's son Alexander

                          KINAU (daughter) m. KEKUANAOA

        ALEXANDER (Kamehameha IV)   LOT (Kamehameha V)
            m. Queen EMMA

At his death in 1872, Lot Kamehameha had not named a successor. The only two known surviving descendants of the Conqueror, Princess Ruth Keelikolani and Princess Bernice Puahi, both refused the crown. Under the Constitution adopted for the kingdom in the reign of Kamehameha III, a successor must then be chosen by vote of the Legislature. The candidates in this election were Prince William Charles Lunalilo and Colonel David

Kalakaua. Lunalilo was chosen, but died after only a year and without having named a successor. In the new election thus made necessary, the candidates were David Kalakaua and Dowager Queen Emma. This time, in 1874, Kalakaua was the victor. His accession established a new dynasty, bearing his name, upon Hawaii's throne.

The family of Kalakaua descended from a high chief, Kepookalani, who was first cousin to Kamehameha I, their mothers having been sisters.

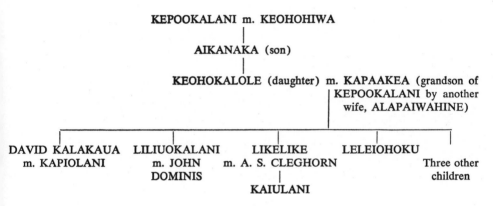

KEPOOKALANI m. KEOHOHIWA

AIKANAKA (son)

KEOHOKALOLE (daughter) m. KAPAAKEA (grandson of KEPOOKALANI by another wife, ALAPAIWAHINE)

DAVID KALAKAUA m. KAPIOLANI

LILIUOKALANI m. JOHN DOMINIS

LIKELIKE m. A. S. CLEGHORN

KAIULANI

LELEIOHOKU

Three other children

BOOK I

Princess in a Garden

I: An Island World

She was to die an American.

Yet the part of the world upon which her eyes first opened—on October 16, 1875—was (although Americans already controlled its economic life) almost in no way like America. It did not stir to dreams of becoming one among fifty closely-knit United States. It was a tiny but proudly independent kingdom, an archipelago of islands strung out at the trade crossroads of the Pacific, like beads on green-blue silk.

Hawaii—the Hawaii with whose destiny Princess Victoria Kaiulani's own was to mingle—had been, at the time of her birth, a civilized kingdom for something less than a century.

Only in 1778 had Captain James Cook, first white man to view the Islands, arrived off Oahu and Kauai. Only in 1795 had the Polynesian military genius Kamehameha defeated a last petty island king to make himself ruler of a united kingdom. Only in 1820 had the earliest New England missionaries brought their "god in a little black box" (the Bible) to a hitherto pagan Hawaii.

But the first three-quarters of the nineteenth century had transformed a colorful kingdom almost beyond recognition. Gone were the hideous carved stone or wooden gods with their grinning shark teeth. Gone, for the most part, were the steep-roofed grass houses. Gone, at least from the surface of Island days, were the often terrifying superstitions and punishments and tabus of earlier

3

times. Five Kamehamehas and two other kings had ruled Hawaii in the interim.

The consulates of a score of nations had become busy offices in Honolulu. Smart carriages rolled along the city streets. Churches lifted serene spires. Ladies attended balls and receptions in velvets from Paris, and government officials wore gold-braided uniforms. Prosperous businesses crowded the downtown district. The waterfront was a forest of masts, as whalers and traders brought wealth to new commercial overlords. France and England each had laid brief, violent hold upon Hawaii and then turned her back to her lawful rulers.

Born of shattering underwater explosions—literally hurled above the waves and then slowly cooled until their crumbled lava soil grew ready for green fertility—these islands became a land of contrasts; a land where black crags jutted along the countless bays and water like jeweled enamel gleamed in the quiet lagoons, where volcanoes still awoke to writhing fire, where snows capped the higher mountains and lush jungle crowded the valleys, where bright flowers and brighter-plumed birds rivaled the ever-present rainbows, and where (on occasion) the pagan voice of a *kahuna* drum still might throb in a lonely night.

Such was the land-in-transition in which, one day in 1851, the Scots lad who was destined to become Kaiulani's father first set foot. The brig *Sisters* had brought him with his ailing father, bound from Auckland to California. But the elder Cleghorn survived only as far as Hawaii. Stranded by his parent's death in the little kingdom of Kamehameha III, and only sixteen years old, Edinburgh-born Archibald began to fend for himself as a humble clerk in a downtown store.

But Hawaii, in addition to being a tropic paradise, was also a land burgeoning with opportunity. Four brief years later, when he was accepted into membership in the exclusive gentlemen's club known as The Mess, Archie Cleghorn already was well on his way toward heading his own importing firm. By the time he had married a vivacious native princess and had helped her brother to become King of Hawaii, his interests occupied impressive headquarters at the corner of Kaahumanu and Queen

Streets in Honolulu—with branches on three outlying islands. He had built himself a handsome house on Emma Street in the city; a house close to the foot of Punchbowl crater and set among tall palms and trim lawns. His new wife was a darling of the little city's gay society, and her entertainments glittered extravagantly through those spacious Emma Street reception halls.

In one of the ground-floor rooms pretty young Mrs. Cleghorn —otherwise Her Royal Highness, Princess Miriam Likelike, third in the direct line of succession—bore her only daughter. Guns fired a salute to inform Honolulu of the arrival of a niece to His Majesty, King Kalakaua. And at four o'clock that October afternoon, all the bells in the city pealed the glad news.

Two months old on her first Christmas Day, the baby was carried from the house on Emma Street in the arms of her nurse, Kahakukaakoi. With Princess Likelike alongside, they rode in the royal carriage to St. Andrew's Episcopal Church. Before a congregation which overflowed the pews, the newest member of the King's family was christened by Bishop Willis—Victoria Kawekiu Lunalilo Kalaninuiahilapalapa Kaiulani. The King, the Queen, and huge, hideous, greatly loved Princess Ruth Keeli-kolani stood as her sponsors, beside a font decorated with white flowers and the inscription: *E ae aku i kalalii liilii e hele mai ana i oʻu nei*—"Suffer little children to come unto me."

Kaiulani wore an elegant cashmere baptismal robe, embroidered in silk. Afterward there was a state reception at the old wooden palace, soon to be demolished in favor of a grander one of stone —"where all," according to the Hawaiian newspaper *Kuokoa,* "could see the new princess. We saw her that afternoon with the finest assembly of people our eyes had ever met." Stationed in the palace grounds, the Royal Hawaiian Band provided music. A feature of their entertainment was a work especially composed for the occasion by their leader, Captain Henri Berger, which he had named "The Kaiulani March."

But the house on Emma Street was not even a memory, as Kaiulani grew older. Many financially comfortable Honolulu residents maintained villas out at suburban Waikiki, four miles beyond the city, where the sea bathing was at its best. Well before their small daughter's birth, the Cleghorns had purchased such a retreat. Originally (as part of the estate of Kaiulani's godmother, Princess Ruth) the area had been called Auaukai. But when its new owners first took possession, Princess Likelike had felt the Manoa Valley breeze which touched this scrap of Waikiki alone; and she had re-named it "cool place," Ainahau.

Sometime during Kaiulani's third year, Archibald Cleghorn sold the mansion in town and moved his family permanently out to Waikiki. Long before this move, he had begun to plant the thousands of botanical specimens which were to make his acres a showplace. Date palms nodded over Ainahau's roofs like stately *kahilis,* and directly in front of the house stood the vast banyan tree from which all other trees of its species in Honolulu were said to be descended. From the very first, Kaiulani made that great tree, with its cluster of central trunks and its wilderness of spreading, twisted branches, her particular domain.

The other trees of Ainahau made a romantic poem when a small girl merely recited their names: mango, cinnamon, teak, camphor, Monterey cypress. One tree from India bore scarlet blossoms shaped like tiger claws. Fourteen varieties of hibiscus bloomed in the gardens, along with shiny-leafed Hawaiian *kamani* trees and sago palms and tawny croton.

Archibald Cleghorn put down an artesian well especially to feed the three lily ponds (one of them artfully shaped like a shamrock) which added drama to his gardens. His peafowl paced the lawns like arrogant soldiers on sentry duty. Several old-style native grass dwellings had dotted the acres before they came into his possession and he left the best among these as a garden house—a fine example of the ancient techniques of construction, although floored now and furnished in more modern fashion.

This was Ainahau. This was a tiny princess's realm within her royal uncle's kingdom. Here, not surprisingly, the household revolved about her. Here, she passed her days first with her nurse, May Leleo, and later with her governess, Miss Barnes. Old May had the fascination of a legend. Her father was said to have been killed by a fall from a horse while seeking the secret burial cave which held the bones of Kamehameha the Conqueror

—a certain sign from the gods that the unknown tomb was not to be violated. But Miss Barnes represented authority.

One of Kaiulani's earliest memories was of a gift that dear "Mama Nui"—her pet name for gigantic Princess Ruth—had sent out to Ainahau. Miss Barnes supervised the polite expression of thanks which a young princess must make.

> Dear Mama Nui [Kaiulani had written]: Thank you for the nice hat you sent me. It fits so nicely Mama wanted it, but I would not let her have it. Thank you for the corn and watermelons, they do taste so good. Are you well? With much love to you from your little girl—Kaiulani.

To this was added a hasty postscript:

> I want you to give Miss Barnes a native name.

In a sequel concerning the gift bonnet, Kaiulani had needed Miss Barnes's best comforting. Equipped with her own full share of royal willfulness, Archibald Cleghorn's daughter nonetheless was ill-armed for any clash of intentions with her imperious mother. From the argument between them about the hat, as from others, she emerged second best. A new letter soon went forth to Princess Ruth, barely masking its small author's outrage:

> Dear Mama Nui: I want another hat. Mama Likelike has taken the hat you sent me. Are you better now. When are you coming home. With much love. From your little girl—Kaiulani.

The greatest delight of those years while she was growing up in her father's garden, coming by gradual stages to understanding of who she was and why she was important in Hawaii, was another gift, a gift from Papa. It had been love at first sight between her and the white saddle pony, Fairy, from the very day Papa brought him home. By the time she was seven, Kaiulani handled the gentle animal expertly. With a mounted groom in attendance, she was permitted to ride the roads around Waikiki, and sometimes to venture farther afield, into the residential sections of the city proper.

A favorite objective for such longer rides was the town house of "Uncle John" Cummins, important in His Majesty's

government. The spreading Cummins house faced its street behind
a fence with two gates, all painted gleaming white. From the larger
gate, nearer town, Kaiulani cantered up a driveway lined with
yellow coreopsis. Occupied though he might be by public affairs,
"Uncle John" never failed to come out to greet her himself. From
Fairy's snowy back, Kaiulani could look down upon him like
an empress upon a favorite courtier.

"Uncle John," she would command, "I want some milk."

And he himself would go to fetch it for her. The milk came
from cows in his own paddock, and Kaiulani was convinced it
was far superior to the milk of lesser cattle—even those that
served Ainahau.

In little else could the world outside her father's gates—with
their stern signs reading *Kapu,* which meant "forbidden"—offer
competition. Here, everyone came to her. The fashionable carriages were always arriving and departing. The suppers and
dances were forever filling the house and its gardens with lanterns
and laughter and music. The proud peacocks staged their endless
vain parades. The servants and Miss Barnes attended to her
every need and wish. Actually, Ainahau *was* the world.

But even such a safe harbor could be invaded by the excitement
of real history. And, when she was seven, came the morning of
her kingly uncle's formal coronation.

2: The Crown of Paradise

A coronation! Although five of her kings slept in royal tombs, and a yet greater one in his secret cave, Hawaii had never before witnessed such an event as this. Nor had there been, until now, real crowns for Hawaii. But "Papa Moi" (as Kaiulani had learned to call Mama's brother, King David Kalakaua, the kingdom's *moi* or chief-of-chiefs) had recently returned from an energetic tour of the world. And he had come home quite determined that his small Polynesian realm must lack none of the majesties he had witnessed abroad. So on February 12, 1883, nine years after he had mounted the throne, his people were to see him crowned.

Although it was a long drive in to the city from Waikiki, the Cleghorn family's carriages rolled between the wide-flung rear gates to Iolani Palace well before noon on this day of days. The handsome new building's light-colored walls, its girdle of verandas and colonnades, its squat cupolas, swung into view beyond rows of majestic palm trees. The sun, a stranger to Honolulu during the past several anxious days, shone overhead like a polished shield.

Already, at the front of the palace, the collecting crowd had become dense. All along the way, the road had been smothered in traffic—people in carriages, people on horseback or thronging the new mule-drawn streetcars, beaming *kanakas* afoot, all of them coronation bound. It seemed to Kaiulani, riding at her

9

mother's side, that the whole island of Oahu must be headed toward the ceremonies.

As the carriages rolled to a halt, she had only an instant to wonder (with a thrill of horror) whether or not an assassin still might lurk somewhere among the smiling faces. Although the danger now supposedly was over, she had heard her elders whispering and she understood.

A plot had been afoot—might still be afoot—to start a public riot during the coronation ceremonies. Political enemies of Papa Moi—and these always seemed to be a certain clique of foreign businessmen in the kingdom—were said to have imported from California one Charles Patrick Carson and to have offered him pay for the unthinkable act of assassinating the white-bearded Premier of the kingdom, Walter Murray Gibson, during the holiday confusion.

But when Carson had arrived in Honolulu a month ago he had discovered that, contrary to what he had been told, the native Hawaiians deeply loved their King. Then he had gone straight to Mr. Gibson's son-in-law at his newspaper office to reveal the whole plot. Forewarned, Papa Moi and his faithful though unpopular Premier had posted police where trouble might erupt. Still, there was a terrible possibility . . .

Apprehensions interrupted, Kaiulani was being lifted down from the carriage and hurried up the palace steps. Once within the palace, she could rush to a long front window overlooking what was going on outside.

The crowd already gathered below seemed to glitter. Officers from all the foreign warships in the harbor had appeared in full regalia—swords, gold braid, and lace. The diplomats looked as dignified as wax mannequins. Their ladies were a flower garden of the latest French and New York fashions. The rich *haole* (or white foreign) families—those who had not remained away because of political differences with Papa Moi—seemed scarcely less impressive. And proudest of all were the dusky Hawaiians, Mama's own people, noble *alii* and commoners alike.

A wide platform had been erected from the palace's front

steps, across the lawns to a handsome pavilion with open sides; a painted, flower-garlanded pavilion in which (under a pointed roof of red, white, and blue stripes) the two throne chairs of crimson and gilt waited. Papa Moi's stood draped in the priceless robe of yellow feathers which had been the august symbol of royalty to an earlier Hawaii knowing nothing of crowns. It had taken many generations to make this cape, since only two golden feathers grew at the breast of each of the rare birds from which they had been taken. Mama's brief but solemn role in the ceremonies would be to lift the cloak from the throne at an appointed moment and drape it over her kingly brother's shoulders.

Kaiulani, peering out from the big window, was screened by the heavy curtain from the gaze of the assemblage. They would have recognized a princess of Hawaii in her delicate, small figure wearing a pale blue silk dress, corded and trimmed with lace—that beautiful new blue dress which matched the hair ribbons catching back black, flowing hair from a cream-skinned, dark-eyed face. If they had caught a glimpse of her, people might have begun to wave—even to applaud. And Mama would have been furious.

Everywhere today one saw the Hawaiian flag, the national colors, flowing out across the sunshine as if the Union Jack and the eight stripes representing the Kingdom's principal islands rejoiced with their nation at the crowning of its King. Now the Royal Hawaiian Band was pouring out over the scene a stirring wash of music. There came as if from nowhere an ancient crone in a flowered *holoku,* who lifted her cracked voice to chant a *mele* praising the achievements of David Kalakaua from cradle to throne and outlining his lineage.

To either side of the long platform, the King's *kahili* bearers stood in double rows, motionless as trees. Their feather standards nodded in the gentle wind on staffs fully ten feet high, rounded columns of plumage massed over stiff, invisible under-structures of straw. Conspicuously shorter, on staffs of sandalwood and tortoise shell, the spotless white feather kahilis personal to the royal family were grouped within the pavilion.

Now the procession was forming in the hall. Dreamlike in her gown of white figured brocade trimmed in pearls—in scarlet satin slippers, in elegant Sarah Bernhardt gloves—Princess Like-like hurried her small daughter to an appointed place in line, where Kaiulani's devoted governess, Miss Barnes, waited to take charge. As the band outside struck up the national anthem, "Hawaii Ponoi," its words composed by Papa Moi himself, some-one thrust flowers into her small hands.

> *Hawaii Ponoi*
> *Nana i kou moi*
> *Kalani Alii*
> *Ke Alii.*
> *Makua lani e*
> *Kamehameha e*
> *Na kaua e pale*
> *Me ka ihe . . .*

> (Hawaii's own true sons
> Be loyal to your chief,
> Your country's liege and lord,
> The Alii.
> Father above us all,
> Kamehameha himself,
> Who guarded in the war
> With his battle spear . . .)

The procession was ready. First the Queen's sisters, Princesses Kekaulike and Poomaikalani; then the chamberlain of the King-dom, Albert Francis Judd; then Kaiulani herself, then Mama and Papa. Uncle John Dominis, governor of Oahu, followed with his wife Aunt Liliu, Mama's elder sister and the heiress apparent, handsome as sculpture in her Paris gown of gold and white. It was made, that gown, in a myriad of tiny puffs, each secured by a miniature golden bird.

Behind Aunt Liliu the glittering line continued. Glancing back, Kaiulani could see the solemn figures of two of her three nearly-grown-up boy cousins by marriage, "Koa" and "Kuhio." Prince David Kawananakoa bore one of the new crowns of Hawaii, and

Prince Jonah Kuhio Kalanianaole the other. Such exquisite crowns! Fashioned of gold taro leaves (for from taro came *poi,* long the chief food of the nation), they were encrusted with rubies, emeralds, diamonds, pearls, and with the polished *kukui* nuts that were once the chief jewelry of the Islands.

Behind the crown-bearers, lesser alii carried the other ceremonial objects to be displayed: the *kapu* sticks, the scepter, the seal ring. So far away that they were scarcely visible waited the altogether wonderful figures of Their Majesties, the Queen's eight ladies-in-waiting gathered behind them all gowned in satin-trimmed black velvet.

Stately music from the park grew louder as the huge palace doors were opened. As the line in the hall began to move in step to it, Kaiulani moved too—out into the brightness and the full public view.

The Marshal of the Kingdom led them, bearing his impressive golden staff of office. Out along the platform leading to the pavilion the brilliant procession advanced. Those not to take actual part in the ceremonies, Kaiulani included, had been drilled to step aside into predesignated positions on the palace *lanai.*

Papa Moi seemed almost a stranger as he paced past, so tall and straight in his spotless white uniform of the King's Guard and his white helmet plumed in red, white, and blue. His black whiskers gleamed magnificently. On his chest flashed Hawaii's Order of Kamehameha and the decorations bestowed upon him by the rulers of Japan, Siam, England, and Portugal. Never beautiful but stately and sweet-faced and every inch a Queen, Mama Moi moved beside him in a regal gown of red velvet created for her by J. Furneaux of London.

The band's music faded. At the pavilion the rector of Saint Andrew's church, the Reverend Mr. Alexander MacIntosh, stepped out like an earthbound angel in his white surplice to read (first in English, then in Hawaiian) a service previously printed and distributed among his listeners.

Ceremony pressed upon ceremony. Chancellor Judd set the Sword of State in the King's hands. Mama played her brief role with the feather cape. The ring was slipped upon Papa Moi's finger. The choir chanted. Hymns were sung. At last came the awesome moment.

Chancellor Judd lifted the King's crown from its cushion and laid it in Kalakaua's hands. Papa Moi grasped it firmly and set it upon his own proud head. In Hawaii, no noble or dignitary stood so high that he might presume to crown his monarch.

But a King might crown a Queen. After yet another prayer, Papa Moi accepted the lesser crown and turned to set it upon the brow of Aunt Kapiolani. A sudden gasp arose from the on-lookers. For Her Majesty's intricate puffs and curls had been piled up without regard for this symbolic act. The crown would not fit into place.

Hastily, her ladies-in-waiting fluttered about the Queen. While Kaiulani watched wide-eyed, while the crowd stood staring, Her Majesty's veil was removed. Her big combs were plucked out of the way, her hairpins worked free. Now Papa Moi lifted the crown once more.

But still it would not fit. At last, just as the waiting grew un-endurable, the King jammed the jeweled headpiece into place by main force. Those nearby said afterward that they had seen the poor Queen wince. But the moment passed. Again "Hawaii Ponoi" rang out across the park. Again Kalakaua moved in pro-cession along the platform. A distant boom of guns aboard men-of-war off the waterfront announced the conclusion of the rites. The choir burst into "Cry Out, O Isles, with Joy!" composed by Premier Gibson especially to honor the great event.

Hawaii's first coronation was over.

Yet the never-to-be-forgotten day had not ended.

As night came on, new crowds began to gather in the palace gardens, which—emptied after the morning's ceremonies—had drowsed through the afternoon's long heat. These evening ar-rivals were special guests. Each had received a heavy card en-graved with a gold crown on a crimson cushion, its message beginning: "The Chamberlain of the Household is commanded by His Majesty to invite . . ."

Kaiulani (whose own invitation rested at home on her dressing table, a precious souvenir) stood primly near the end of the receiving line. In first position stood the King, dashingly handsome in a fresh white uniform, this one trimmed in gold and finished off with ornamental sword and scarlet sash. Mama Moi stood beside him, laced into a tight European gown of heavy velvet which seemed to stifle her.

Then came Aunt Liliu, regal and polished and popular—her gown another Paris importation of crimson satin, heavily embroidered, which admiring whispers conceded to be the most elegant costume yet seen in Honolulu. But to Kaiulani's way of thinking, no other lady in the garden could hold a candle to Mama, whose dress was made of a shimmery moonstone-hued silk someone had called moonlight-on-the-lake. On Mama, it was as beautiful as it sounded. Likelike's dance card filled swiftly. Everyone, gentlemen in particular, adored the vivacious younger sister of the King.

Although Kaiulani was considered far too young for dancing, a twin of Mama's dance card hung at her wrist, another souvenir. Upon its cover, within a thick gold border, was emblazoned the crown again; and that noble phrase which during the reign of Kamehameha III had become Hawaii's motto: *Ua mau ke ea o ka aina i ka pono,* which meant "The life of the land is perpetuated in righteousness." On two narrow inside pages, like gay music itself, ran the "Order of Dances": waltz . . . lancers . . . polka . . .

Each guest, moving forward as his name was announced, bowed deeply before Their Majesties. Their bows to Mama and Aunt Liliu, and to Kaiulani, while not so sweeping, were respectful and friendly. The line seemed endless. "Princess . . ." voices kept murmuring. And: "Your Highness . . ."

Red baize cushioned the pumps of the crowd flowing up and down the palace steps. Windows blazed with the new electric lights that Papa Moi had feared might not be installed in time for his coronation. Colored lanterns were strung everywhere. The dancing began at last, music augmenting the laughter. There had been no thought of rain, yet suddenly it came in a bright, brisk pattering on the canvas canopy overhead. Water sluiced down, and was blown in at the tent's open sides.

The red baize on the open stairs quickly became sodden, its scarlet turned black. Ladies in filmy frocks and satin slippers began to squeal in dismay. Then two men in uniforms of the Palace Guard came running down the steps, carrying a chair between them. One lady, braver than the rest, accepted their offer to carry her. Back up the steps she was whisked, the guardsmen still running until they could set her down under cover.

Other stalwart chair teams went into action. Up and down the rain-swept stairs they raced. Almost before she realized what was happening, Kaiulani found herself being borne aloft by one of them. Scarcely had she felt the rain on her face before she was safe on the dry lanai. As she glanced back, the big dancing tent in the garden seemed almost empty.

But the throne room had been opened up to receive the dancers. Music lifted anew, this time inside the palace, and across the polished floor the guests spun all the merrier for their brief flurry. Never until tonight had Kaiulani been permitted to stay up so late. But then, never before had Hawaii celebrated at a coronation ball.

3: Family Circle

The days of celebration following the coronation wore themselves out, warming Ainahau in a golden afterglow.

During the spring following the coronation, the Cleghorn family left Waikiki only once, to make a visit to the Big Island, Hawaii, for what seemed to Kaiulani a most exciting purpose. A huge gold-and-bronze statue of Kamehameha the Great was dedicated at Kohala, the hamlet where the Conqueror had been born, and Mama Likelike was the person chosen to unveil it. The Cleghorns had scarcely returned to Ainahau before unwelcome news followed them home. On the Big Island they just had visited, old Princess Ruth—long ailing—had died. The word reached them just past mid-May. And a few days later, the body of the massive old princess was returned to Oahu to lie in state.

"Mama Nui" had been dearly loved by the child she left behind. The vast old bosom had been a refuge, the raddled old face a blessing. And now, Kaiulani would know them no more. The wonderful old woman was gone, and this emptiness she left behind was what death really meant.

Within the walls of the old princess's mansion on Emma Street, a succession of sad ceremonies spun themselves out. Old chanters came out of the hills to raise their voices in the meles sacred to the departed one; for no high-born infant saw the light in old Hawaii without being accorded his special chants to describe the event. They were performed again when he died, a plaintive threnody of remembrance.

It also was the custom for all alii of the same rank as the one lost to the nation to gather at the place of the lying-in-state, there to remain until the funeral. So Mama Likelike, along with a handful of others, took up residence on Emma Street; and for the three weeks prescribed by this ritual, Ainahau seemed mournfully empty.

The things that welded together the household at Ainahau in normal times—and normal times did, of course, return—were not ties of blood alone. Other interests bound it to a circle of relatives mostly royal, and to the world outside.

There was music, for example. Mama's maternal great-grandmother had been Ululani, one of Hawaii's great *haku mele,* or poets. Her genius had blossomed again in all four of the brothers and sisters who came to be the nation's royal family. Each of the four had founded a club of singers, who contested with one another. Each had composed original music. Aunt Liliu's "Aloha Oe" was by far the most famous of these compositions, even including Papa Moi's proud "Hawaii Ponoi." Among the songs that Mama Likelike had written, Kaiulani's favorite was the one called "Maikai Waipio," which described a place she knew and loved:

> *Maikai Waipio alolua i na pali*
>   (Beautiful Waipio with opposing cliffs)
> *E poai a puni ana a hapa nae makai*
>   (Hemmed in by girdling cliffs facing seaward)
> *Maemae ka pua i ka holo ae a ka wai*
>   (Pure are the flowers growing beside the water)
> *Ua enaena i ka la, mohala i na pali*
>   (Warmed by the sun, blooming in the cliffs)
> *Hoihoi ka piina o Koaekea*
>   (Delightful the ascent to Koaekea)
> *Pii no hoomaha i ka Holokuaiwa.*
>   (An ascent to the resting-place of Holokuaiwa).

Music always played an important role at Ainahau. So, too, did Papa's eminence as a leading business figure in the community. Kaiulani was still very young when Papa first instructed her in what it meant to be a stockholder.

That exclusive gentlemen's club first named The Mess had later become the British Club. At the time it applied to the Privy Council for a charter of incorporation, Papa was its president. He showed Kaiulani the application. "The Capital of said Corporation shall be Six Thousand dollars, divided into one hundred and twenty shares. . . ." And among the shareholders of record, one of only two feminine names listed, was Kaiulani's, as owner of two shares! For anyone only seven years old, it was quite a distinction to possess business holdings.

Papa himself, of course, stood at the center of the family group, tall and dignified. Also on the Cleghorn side, not resident at Ainahau but frequent visitors, were Kaiulani's three half-sisters, Helen and Rosie and Annie. During those dim years while (presumably) Papa had been waiting for a much younger Mama to grow up and marry him, he once before had fallen in love. His Elizabeth had given him three daughters. Mama always welcomed them to Ainahau as if they were her own, and their visits were happily anticipated. Helen was Mrs. James Harbottle Boyd. Rosie was Mrs. James Robertson. But Annie was fifteen and still, like Kaiulani herself, a "Miss Cleghorn."

As was natural, Mama's kinfolk stood more in the public eye. The King, her brother, moved always in a spotlight. And when he was away from home—as on his grand tour around the world, two years before—attention merely shifted to his Regent, Aunt Liliu.

Papa Moi had still been absent on that grand tour, Kaiulani could remember, when Honolulu received the sad news of the death of America's President, James A. Garfield, who had been shot by an assassin in a railroad station nine weeks before. Suddenly, the city was draped in mourning. But at the time, another matter of seemingly equal importance had competed for Kaiulani's attention. As Princess Regent, Aunt Liliu was about to set out on a tour of state around the island of Oahu; and Mama Likelike and Kaiulani (with Miss Barnes, of course) were to accompany her!

The party of carriages and mounted riders had made a first stop at Waimanalo, the country estate of "Uncle John" Cummins. To be invited to Waimanalo for goat-shooting was to enjoy the very finest of Island welcomes. It was the custom of "Uncle John" to ferry his guests to windward Oahu aboard his private steamer, the *Waimanalo*. Scores of his friends were entertained at banquets served in the ancient style.

Among the grass houses scattered through the Cummins grounds was one set apart exclusively as Kaiulani's own, and before it were planted the gilded kapu sticks proclaiming the residence of a high alii. When Uncle John had first set up his new flagpole nearby, Kaiulani had raised the beautiful Hawaiian standard to flutter from its top, and had christened it with a bottle of champagne. So she knew Waimanalo well.

Refreshed after a brief rest there, the party moved on for the night to Maunawili, the mountain retreat of Kaiulani's half-sister Helen and Helen's husband, James Boyd. Weary from excitement, Kaiulani soon fell asleep. But for her elders, the entertainment had lasted late, a gay prelude for disaster to come.

Early next morning, as the cavalcade descended the mountain, Aunt Liliu was flung from her carriage and was so badly injured that she had to be carried down by litter to the flats. There a wagon stood ready to transport her to the Cummins' private steamer. Darkness fell before the little *Waimanalo* had crept across Honolulu harbor to dock at the foot of Fort Street, where silent crowds had gathered in the moonlight.

The stretcher was carried ashore by soldiers, and along the blocks to Washington Place, the big white-pillared Dominis home on Beretania Street. Even now Kaiulani could remember her terror at the shops and houses past which they had moved, still festooned in the somber crepe put up for President Garfield. For long weeks, the shadow of Aunt Liliu's accident tarnished every event at Ainahau. Mama drove daily in to the city to sit at her sister's bedside, sometimes taking Kaiulani with her.

Until then, for Kaiulani, visits to Washington Place had been gala outings. The big mansion—built decades earlier by Uncle John's father, Captain Dominis of New England, as a home for his wife, Mary, and his son, John Owen—had a romantic and mysterious story. Soon after his house was completed, the captain had sailed for China on a trading journey. But once his brig *Nielsen* had cleared Honolulu harbor on a bright August day, she was never heard of again.

Later, the widow decided to accept a roomer in the big place where she and her son roamed like shadows. Her tenant was the United States Commissioner to Honolulu. He soon secured Mrs. Dominis's permission to name after his homeland's great hero, George Washington, the mansion which thus was transformed into an American Legation.

After her son grew up and married the young chiefess then known as Lydia Liliu Kapaakea, the bride and groom came there to live. Mama Likelike had become Papa's bride in the Dominis house on September 22, 1870, with King Lot Kamehameha signing the register as a witness. And Mrs. Mary Dominis (although she was now a very old lady) still presided over Washington Place.

Aunt Liliu's accident did not prove as drastic as that somber crepe had suggested to a frightened child. Gradually, from bed and then from chair, the Princess Regent was able to resume some of her temporary responsibilities. And then the King returned— and such a welcome that had been! Arches everywhere! Flowers everywhere! Flags and crowds everywhere!

Kaiulani could not say, even these years afterward, just how she had become aware that a certain event of the King's journey affected her personally. Her knowledge of it seemed to have come a scrap at a time. But the total, pieced together, was startling. She never had thought seriously that someday she would be grown up like Mama and a married lady. But Kalakaua must have thought about it.

The thing that concerned Kaiulani had happened during his visit to Japan. There, in spite of the watchful eye kept upon him by members of the Missionary set who traveled with the party, Papa Moi had contrived an informal private interview with the Mikado. During the previous state ceremonies with which he had been honored, Mama's brother had been much impressed with a fifteen-year-old Japanese prince serving as a cadet at the Imperial Naval College. He had made the suggestion that this youth be betrothed to the little Princess of Hawaii, thus establishing a Japanese protectorate over the Islands.

Such an arrangement would have checkmated the plans of certain haole businessmen muttering threats of annexing Hawaii to their own United States. But the Mikado had felt that this suggestion required further consideration. Nothing had been settled, not even when, considerably later, Lord Michinori Nagasaki, master of ceremonies to the Mikado, had paid a state visit to the kingdom. Kaiulani's alarm then had been quieted by Papa's reports that His Lordship's concern was with the possible importation of Japanese laborers to work Hawaii's big sugar plantations. Except that he brought her gifts of beautiful kimonos and rolls of rare silk, the government's guest might never have heard of a Princess Kaiulani.

And so, to this very spring of Papa Moi's coronation, no foreign prince had been added to the intimate family circle at Ainahau.

4: Miss Gardinier

Outsiders were almost as much a part of life at Ainahau as were the family and their employees. Frequently, little girls were fetched out to Waikiki to play with Kaiulani, most of them the daughters of Mama's fashionable friends in the city. Among these, Elsie Jaeger was a special favorite. Small and timid, Elsie was frightened speechless by the royal rages which sometimes flared at Ainahau.

Mama Likelike—delicately made and stylish and extraordinarily pretty—had a vivacity and charm which since her early girlhood had captivated haoles quite as much as Hawaiians. Her willfulness and pride—sometimes very close to selfishness—somehow did not seem to make her any less attractive.

But Mama's temper could be as violent as her smiles were charming; and Kaiulani's own was a miniature copy of the original, although generally held under better control. Once Elsie had seen Mama use her whip on a groom because he had not properly polished her beautiful carriage. Small wonder she was fearful!

On one particular day Kaiulani, seated in the huge banyan tree, was playing that she was the Great Queen of all Hawaii. She decreed that her young playmates all prostrate themselves before her, as the natives of pre-missionary times always had done in the presence of royalty. All the children except Elsie, herself of alii blood, scrambled to obey. The two little girls (Kaiulani angered by Elsie's refusal, Elsie by Kaiulani's anger) shrilled at each other like two of the Cleghorn peafowl. At last, badgered beyond thought of consequences, Elsie snatched up a stick and hurled it at her tree-enthroned tormentor. To her horror, the missile struck Kaiulani just above one eye, and blood seeped from a long scratch.

The moment of trantrum passed as quickly as one of Hawaii's sudden showers, and within minutes the two were playing peaceably together. Their disagreement was long forgotten before they were summoned in to lunch. But here, to Elsie's terror, it was abruptly recalled. At the head of her table, Princess Likelike suddenly noticed the mark on her beloved daughter's temple. She leaned forward in motherly concern.

"Kaiulani, where did you get that?"

For Elsie, the dining room was suddenly a dungeon. Hawaiians of only two generations previous had been strangled for daring to cross a king's shadow. The likelihood of what might happen here, once Likelike's famous rage had been aroused, was too frightful to imagine.

But Kaiulani, eyes bright with mischief, was answering demurely. "I fell down, Mama." The danger passed, leaving poor Elsie limp. . . .

Little girls did well enough as companions. But rarer and even more eagerly awaited were visits from "the boys." By this term the household did not mean just *any* boys, but rather three in particular, all impressively older than Kaiulani, old enough to be heroes rather than playmates. The gulf between eight and fifteen, which was Koa's awesome age—or fourteen, which was Edward's, or even twelve, which was Kuhio's—was like the gulf between being a boy or a girl.

The trio, who like herself had taken part in Papa Moi's recent coronation, were bound to Ainahau by links an outsider might find confusing.

They were known to Honolulu, collectively, as "the young princes." Their mother had been a sister to Queen Kapiolani. But they also were descended from King Keawe of Hawaii, and thus were distant cousins to Papa Moi and Mama Likelike as well.

Her Majesty had adopted Koa (David Kawananakoa) and Kuhio (Jonah Kuhio Kalanianaole), whom people sometimes called Prince Cupid. Her Royal Highness, Princess Poomaikalani, had adopted the middle brother, Edward Abel Keliiahoui. So their family position as foster sons forged yet another royal tie. Kaiulani adored them, all three.

During the summer of 1883, real grief struck savagely and without warning at her garden world. Impossible, incredible, unbearable as it seemed, dear Miss Barnes died. Suddenly, here were days upon days to be lived through without her governess's familiar presence. Even rides on Fairy were of little comfort. The house seemed empty, gripped by a stillness that the shrill cries of the peacocks could not really break.

As the months wore on, as 1884 began, Papa spoke more and more often of Mr. Lorrin A. Thurston. Kaiulani always had known, of course, who Mr. Thurston was—a young lawyer in the city whose family had been part of the very first band of missionaries to come to Hawaii from New England in 1820. Thurston was a name familiar to everyone in the Islands. But the present representative of the clan lately had given up the law to edit the *Bulletin,* a local newspaper which the sugar planters had taken over to help their established *Gazette* to influence public views in opposition to the King's party.

The main target for haole editorials seemed always to be stately, bearded Mr. Gibson. It was difficult to understand why the foreign businessmen hated him so, merely because he was unwaveringly loyal to a king who was their own king also. Yet for anyone who bore Walter Murray Gibson any friendship whatever, their enmity was unrelenting. In the face of it, Papa resigned his own position on the government's Board of Education—rather than endure their anti-Gibson blocking of every effort toward better public schooling for the native Hawaiians.

Despite these undercurrents of politics, the surface of life in Honolulu and at Waikiki continued in a pleasant pattern. In June, His Royal Highness Prince Oskar of Sweden arrived on a visit. Mama Likelike and Aunt Liliu grew breathless with preparations for entertaining the distinguished foreigner. A grand ball was given at Iolani Palace, where the bright uniforms of the men and the lavish gowns of the ladies were reflected until dawn in the throne room's long mirrors. As Premier, Mr. Gibson gave another fine ball at his private residence. The "Old Queen," Emma, widow of King Kamehameha IV, threw open her country place at Waikiki for a sumptuous *luau,* with the best singers and hula dancers in all the Islands. Such of these events as Kaiulani was permitted to attend seemed to her to rival in splendor the coronation itself. Yet privately she was convinced that His Highness would have had more fun at one of Mama's famous informal croquet parties.

This stylish new game had lately become the rage in Honolulu, largely thanks to Mama's enthusiastic devotion to it. At Ainahau, there were afternoon gatherings at which the guests grew so excited over their sport that it continued on long after dark. Each player made the rounds holding a blazing torch in one hand and a mallet in the other; bustles bobbed, jewels glittered, laces and feathers blew in the Manoa breeze. Minister Sam Wilder's popular daughter Laura was the undisputed champion in these croquet contests. She could go completely around the course in a single turn, driving her ball through each wicket as it came and hitting the "home" stake at the finish.

As 1885 began, the labor future of the kingdom was the real stake in hotly renewed hostilities between Papa Moi and the missionaries. The King was opposed to flooding the country with cheap coolie labor used to living conditions which his Hawaiians never would accept for themselves. The sugar planters intended to get the cheapest workers possible, regardless of any future ill effect upon Hawaii.

Despite an increasing awareness of this grim struggle, Kaiulani still was young enough to find the latest change in her life at Ainahau far more engrossing. She was to have a new governess!

Mama Likelike had asked her American friend, Mrs. George Wallace, wife of the rector at St. Andrew's, to recommend a successor for Miss Barnes; and Mrs. Wallace had undertaken negotiations with a young friend of hers back in the States.

Miss Gertrude Gardinier had been a teacher in the Parish School at Canandaigua, New York. The ship which brought her to Hawaii made harbor on the eighth of May. But it was not Miss Gardinier's intention to take up her new duties immediately upon landing. Instead, she was looking forward to a considerable visit at the home of the Wallaces.

Mama had other plans. The very afternoon of Miss Gardinier's arrival (while Kaiulani remained behind at Ainahau, literally quivering with suspense) Mama drove her smart little carriage to the Wallace home to call upon the governess-to-be. Daylight was fading before the carriage, returning, rolled between the Cleghorn gates and up the driveway.

From her bedroom, Kaiulani heard them coming into the large salon off the front veranda. Mama was acting as a guide, and saying, "Miss Gardinier, this is Kaiulani's and your reception room. . . ." Heels clicked on polished flooring as the two unseen ladies inspected the rest of the suite; the two connected bedrooms with their dressing rooms, leading off the salon.

Afterward, describing the first meeting of her daughter and Miss Gardinier, Mama was fond of telling her friends that it was mutual love at first sight. Certainly, that hour teacher and pupil spent together was a happy time of discovery for each of them.

Dinner was announced in the large lanai, really the heart of life at Ainahau, while Miss Gardinier still admired the wealth of framed pictures on the walls and Papa's library cases overflowing with valuable books. As they moved to the table, Papa (home from his office in the city in time to greet Miss Gardinier with his habitual elegant courtesy) took his customary place at its head. Mama sat on his right, with Kaiulani next to her and Miss Gardinier—as pretty as any of the paintings she had been admiring—on his left. This was always to be the seating arrangement for their informal family meals. From the table one could look out upon a full sweep of the beautiful grounds, in which the house itself sat as a surprisingly modest island.

Conversation centered mostly upon their guest's recent journey from the Atlantic seaboard, and she chattered entertainingly about people she had met along her way. Dinner was long over before the Reverend and Mrs. Wallace arrived to reclaim their house guest.

With Mama, any show of patience was merely a charming pretense. She never permitted something she wanted to be long delayed in coming to her. Not many days had passed before her carriage was again at the Wallaces' door. Since a request from royalty was in effect a command, Miss Gardinier reluctantly agreed to take leave of Mrs. Wallace. The carriage returned to Waikiki with two passengers. Another carriage, promptly dispatched by the Princess, fetched back Miss Gardinier's trunks. While these were being unpacked, Kaiulani watched wide-eyed as each new gown of the latest New York style appeared. She also took great interest in the photographs of Miss Gardinier's family—a mother and a pleasant-looking brother, Robert.

Formal studies were postponed for the first week, while Kaiulani and Miss Gardinier became firm friends. Kaiulani enjoyed the newcomer's astonishment at the full array of her given names. "Victoria Kawekiu Lunalilo Kalaninuiahilapalapa Kaiulani Cleghorn! The Victoria is after Queen Victoria of England. Kaiulani is my own name—it means 'Child of heaven,' and it belonged to Mama's sister who died. The other names are for alii, our high chiefs, and of course the Cleghorn is Papa's name."

Fearing lest Miss Gardinier grow homesick, her pupil decided almost at once to make friends with the owners of the faces on the bureau, the family her pretty mentor had left behind. If they thought well of her royal charge, they might not urge Miss Gardinier to return to them. So to the mother she sent a silver bracelet; to the brother, Robert, a tie pin made of a shell. And she wrote a letter:

Dear Mrs. Gardinier:

I thought I would write you a letter. Miss Gardinier and I went to Honolulu this morning. It has been raining today, but is clearing up now. I had a nice sea bath today. Miss Gardinier would not venture in this morning. I am going to study very hard and try to learn my lessons well, and then I hope to come to the States some day and visit you. I will send you my picture when I have some taken. Miss Gardinier and I are going to ride horseback some day when she learns to. I have a pretty little pony of my own and I am not afraid to ride it. My pony is only four years old, and I am nine years old. Goodbye, from

Kaiulani Cleghorn

Miss Gardinier, also, wrote home about the family at Ainahau of which she had become a part. Her pupil was described to her family as, "the fragile, *spirituelle* type, but very vivacious, with beautiful, large, expressive dark eyes. She proves affectionate, high-spirited, at times quite willful, though usually reasonable and very impulsive and generous." Mr. Cleghorn was reported to be "a man of dignified presence, a genial host, devoted to his family and home, and always a most courteous gentleman." Princess Likelike, the distant Gardiniers learned, was "small, graceful and stylish with pretty dimpled arms and hands. She has an imperious and impulsive nature and is considered quite haughty by some, but she is very genial in her home and is always most thoughtful and considerate of those she likes. . . ."

At the time of Miss Gardinier's arrival, the nation was saddened by the death of the "Old Queen," Emma, who with her kingly husband had won the people's adoration by going from door to door to beg funds for building Queen's Hospital to care for sick Hawaiians. May 17 was set for her funeral.

Callers at Ainahau expressed considerable displeasure with the arrangements being made for the ceremony. The Dowager had lain in state, at first, in her own beloved home up Nuuanu Valley. But then those in charge, claiming that this residence was not large enough to accommodate the crowd expected at the funeral, had removed the body to the stone church at Kawaiahao.

Although Kawaiahao was called "the Westminster Abbey of Hawaii," many—including Aunt Liliu—were angry. Queen Emma not only had been a member of the Episcopal church, St. Andrew's, but even—with her husband—had been largely responsible for inviting the first Anglican clergy to Honolulu. This ignoring of the Queen's church, also attended by all the present royal family, offended Aunt Liliu greatly.

The funeral itself mollified the alii somewhat, for Bishop Willis of the English church was there in the Congregational pulpit to read the service. The pomp and solemnity of the long procession unwinding from Kawaiahao to the Royal Mausoleum in Nuuanu were all one could ask.

The day was of importance to Kaiulani herself because she attended the services in the company of the King. As if he wished to impress upon all onlookers the fact that this slim little girl was a personage of importance in his kingdom, and stood directly in the line of succession, Papa Moi kept her at his side throughout the whole long Sunday. She would have enjoyed this more had the grief of the crowd not pressed in upon her. Later, back at Ainahau, she wrote to Queen Kapiolani of her distress, in an outpouring full of spellings of which Miss Gardinier could scarcely approve:

My Dear Auntie:

Papa Moi and I have just come from the frunral of the old queen. We did not see you there after the parade. Papa says I must write and thank you for the flowers you gave me and the nice little ring.

I do not like frunrals they are sad, and all the noise that the kanakers make scares me something bad. Aunty will you and the Moi Alii come and see me some time soon?

I must play just a bit more and then my govruness makes me take my afternoon rest, so that I will grow big and strong and be a good girl.

Love to you and the King from
Kaiulani

With summer's arrival, Kaiulani no longer lacked company on her daily rides. Miss Gardinier had learned to handle the saddle horse which had been provided for her, in addition to a carriage-and-driver for more formal occasions. They looked forward most of all to their Sunday rides. Early, very early, their horses would be led around to the door. Sometimes their destination would be Pearl City, sometimes the race track at Kapiolani Park. But more usually they veered toward Diamond Head and the Lookout Station there tended by "Diamond Head Charlie" Peterson.

The hour being too early for breakfast, they would each drink a glass of warm milk before leaving Ainahau, and when they reached the station on its high slope Charlie would have coffee waiting. The first time Miss Gardinier went, the lookout offered apologies for having nothing but "sea biscuits" to go with the coffee; and Kaiulani's dark eyes sparkled a dare as she watched a large, rock-hard wafer offered to her governess.

Well aware that she was being tested, Miss Gardinier bit into it at risk to her teeth. But the biscuit proved to have a grim sort of appeal all its own, and on future visits she generally downed a portion. Their homeward trek would begin while the hour still was early, to allow time for gathering sponges or pretty shells along the shore—treasures which beaming attendants, riding behind, then would carry for them.

The rest of Sunday followed a well-established pattern.

After breakfast, regardless of weather, Archibald Cleghorn's household attended services in the city at St. Andrew's. Afterward, they sometimes were invited to lunch with Aunt Liliu at Washington Place, or to the homes of various friends. But more often they returned to Ainahau for a two-o'clock Sunday dinner. Then came long siestas in the shade of the great banyan.

Under the vast tree Kaiulani had her Bible and catechism lessons—and Miss Gardinier found a pupil well versed in both. Later in the afternoon, informal visitors would begin to arrive, swelling the family group. Sprightly conversation, singing, and music would follow as the never-failing Cleghorn hospitality worked its charm.

Although it held to a set schedule in many respects, the weekday routine was less rigidly patterned. After breakfast came lessons and music practice, neither of which Miss Gardinier would stint. The morning might be rounded off with a swim at Waikiki beach, just beyond the gardens and villas across the road; or with surfing, or an occasional drive.

These drives, of course, entailed special responsibility for a princess. Almost from the first day when her parents had let her ride with them past the gates of Ainahau, Kaiulani had been aware that glances followed their progress with more than ordinary interest. She was not permitted to ride as other children might, either oblivious to stares or returning them with an equal curiosity. Instead, she was carefully trained in *haawi ke aloha*— the art of bowing graciously to whomever she might meet; and it had been early impressed upon her that she must never fail in this. Thus recognized, many a stranger she passed on her drives would gape after the fleet, gleaming Cleghorn carriage and murmur, *"Auwe! Ke alii no paha kela!"* ("Why! That must have been the chiefess!")

Afternoons were likely to be devoted to the social training which was a serious part of a princess's education. There were lunches, luaus at the palace, receptions and official picnics, and college and school commencements, at which Kaiulani must appear as a representative of the royal family. If a theatrical company passing through the port, bound for Australia or San Francisco, debarked to perform at the Opera House, Kaiulani and Miss Gardinier attended its matinees—in the King's box. Once (ineffable delight!) there was a circus to be marveled at. Almost as exciting were "Mlle. Garetta with her flock of trained pigeons, doves, monkeys and dogs"; or minstrel shows; or mind readers; or "Miss Mary Cameron, the Human Serpent."

A thing which Miss Gardinier seemed to view with surprise was that servants could be summoned whenever needed. Kaiulani's own personal maid, faithful Kanoah, was always within call when her services were required. One such moment occurred during the very first week of lessons, when Kaiulani accidentally dropped her spelling book. It lay on the floor at her feet, she making no move to pick it up, until Miss Gardinier glanced at her inquiringly.

"I cannot pick it up, Miss Gardinier," Kaiulani explained, a lifetime of training behind her unconscious young arrogance. "You see, I am a princess. And princesses cannot stoop."

"Very well, Kaiulani," Miss Gardinier replied, after a moment of thought. "But, as your governess, I cannot pick it up for you."

Admitting the logic of the argument, Kaiulani graciously

tapped the bell beside her. Like a darting bird, the waiting Kanoah came into the room, retrieved the book, and respectfully handed it to her small mistress. As the maid backed away, the lesson was resumed. After this, it was an understood thing. If a book or handkerchief was dropped, if a glass of water was desired, the bell spoke and Kanoah appeared from nowhere to perform the required service.

Kaiulani's high station was additionally apparent when formal calls were required of her, under Miss Gardinier's chaperonage. The two would set forth from Ainahau in a special carriage made entirely of tortoise shell, which had been the gift of an Eastern queen to the royal family. The horses' harness was all of gilt and the reins of the supplest white leather. The driver perched on a narrow elevated seat behind his two charges, immaculate in black livery and white gloves.

Young and pretty, Miss Gardinier quickly attracted the attention of social Honolulu. Almost as often as Mama (although not with the same royal fanfare) she was invited to the really important events of the capital. It was difficult to imagine (although Kaiulani never, never could be disloyal to the memory of beloved Miss Barnes) a more satisfactory governess!

5: A Difference in Birthdays

As that summer of 1885 ended, Miss Gardinier grew sufficiently concerned about Kaiulani's increasing listlessness to take the matter to Princess Likelike. She suggested that Kaiulani might benefit from a change of climate. Mama agreed, and in September she and Kaiulani, together with Miss Gardinier and Papa's daughter Rosie Robertson and Mrs. George Beckley and several servants, sailed on the steamer *W. G. Hall* for Hawaii, the Big Island.

Mama was particularly beloved on Hawaii, both because of her years as its governor and because her childhood had been spent there. She owned a lovely vacation cottage at Kaawaloa, near Kealekekua Bay. Here the ladies from Honolulu made themselves comfortable, as soon as their steamer had anchored offshore and they had been carried in by canoe. It was a beautiful spot for relaxation and included a small bathing pool filled with achingly cold water where Kaiulani loved to swim.

It had been agreed that lessons would be forgotten for the holiday. So Miss Gardinier was present more in the role of an older friend to Kaiaulani than as a preceptress. The days were a succession of canoe trips, horseback rides, singing, luaus, and sun-bathing on the great rocks. Gaiety often continued into the evening, with torchlight fishing parties to gather sea urchins and *opehe* for Likelike's table.

One of Kaiulani's special delights at Kaawaloa was to watch

for the daily parade of the sharks. Each afternoon precisely at
five o'clock, so punctually that a watch might be set by them,
a line of the huge creatures would pass the rocks on their way
to sea caves where they gathered for the night. Their sinister
dorsal fins, jutting from the water, cut the waves in perfect
procession; and it was frightening to think what they had meant
in times less than a century earlier.

Back then, when king and court gathered at the water line,
the monsters would be driven into shallows within the reef where
they could not turn over. Here they were mounted by skilled
gladiators armed with long poles, who would joust in the effort
to tip each other into the water. Once submerged, a luckless loser
would be within reach of the rending teeth. This gruesome sport
(so like the combat of men and lions in ancient Rome) had been
abandoned long ago. But the sharks remained.

Less terrifying, yet of equal fascination, were the beautiful
rainbows—often as many as five at one time—which on this
particular scrap of the Kona coast arched color over the mountains. Here it was Kaiulani's turn to become teacher, as she informed Miss Gardinier that the brilliant concentration of rainbows in the area was in honor of the many High Chiefs buried
in lost caves along the rugged coast. Old legends claimed that
the heavenly arches were the trail followed by Lono, chief among
the Polynesian deities. The very name of the bay—Kealekekua
—meant, in Hawaiian, "the pathway of the gods."

Once the party had settled in comfortably at Kaawaloa, a
series of visits began to the ranches and homes of Big Island
friends. Local supporters of the monarchy were eager to welcome
its youngest representative, and invitations poured in. Most of
the estates lay back in mountain country, and to get to them it
was necessary to travel precipitous trails on horseback. The
usual party included a guide and perhaps two servants to tend
to the luggage. Such travel, primitive by any standard, was down-
right adventuresome by contrast to the carriages of Honolulu.

At Kaawaloa, Kaiulani passed her tenth birthday. The luau
Mama arranged was to be so elaborate that a new lanai had to
be erected especially for the event. Early on the birthday morning,

Kaiulani and Miss Gardinier took their places on this wide new veranda. And before the sun was high, the Hawaiians began arriving.

As each native subject drew near he knelt before his Princess, reverently kissed her hand, and then presented his gift. Out of the mountains and up from the coastal flats they came, a ceaseless stream along the road, some on horseback, some straddling donkeys, and many afoot. The Big Island's foreign colony joined their Polynesian neighbors at the luau. Always at her best when entertaining, Princess Likelike had outdone herself. In Kaiulani's honor, chanters offered Hawaiian meles which included a special birthday tribute.

Among the haole guests were the government physician for South Kona, a Doctor Baker, and his wife and small son. The doctor had composed as his contribution to the feast an acrostic poem which spelled out the letters of her first name in its line initials:

> V alleys and mountains, the lakes and woods,
> I nvited their denizens, the true and the good;
> C alled aloud to them to come over and see
> T he blessings provided by true liberty.
> O nward they came in the greatest of glee,
> R ejoicing and happy as creatures could be.
> I ncreased was the joy as each one could see
> A Princess among them—Kaiulani.

The poem was further inscribed: "To H.R.H. Princess Kaiulani, from one who wishes her every blessing that may be for her good. That you may be happier every year is the wish of your servant Brooks O. Baker, 16th of October, 1885. . . ."

The celebration thus begun at Kaawaloa continued with much gaiety and feasting right up to the hour when the steamer which was to carry them home to Honolulu anchored offshore. Next morning, as they neared Oahu, the King's yacht came out to put aboard the larger vessel friends laden with flower *leis*. The shore battery fired salutes, and Kaiulani quickly picked out Papa's dignified figure awaiting them among the waving handkerchiefs on the wharf.

And still the birthday celebration was not over.

At Ainahau, the King and Queen themselves waited at the center of a gay party gathered to greet the returning travelers. Several ladies had come out from the city for the special purpose of presenting their small Princess with her own birthday flag—a handsome banner of red silk with a white center, upon which the coat-of-arms of the Kalakaua Dynasty, together with a cross, had been embroidered. Of all the tributes she had received, this one seemed to Kaiulani the most wonderful.

Within days of their return, the old routines at Ainahau had been resumed. Miss Gardinier had started reading aloud *The Life of Queen Victoria* to her Brittanic Majesty's small namesake; and she and Kaiulani were deep in discussions about this great friend of Hawaii.

Thus reading together, they came to the description of a morning when a youthful Victoria refused to practice her music. She had marched to the piano, locked it, slipped the key into her pocket, and said to her instructor, "You see, I am mistress of the situation here!"

"Now, Miss Gardinier," murmured Kaiulani, the beginnings of challenge sparkling in her eyes, "If *I* were to treat *you* like that—"

Again knowing she was being tested, Miss Gardinier moved to the piano on the wide lanai, locked the instrument's lid, and pocketed the key. She turned back, smiling. "But that could not happen, my dear, because *I* am already mistress of the situation here." Caught in her feint at independence, Kaiulani had the grace to laugh.

One happy change which occurred soon after their return was in the matter of daily costume. Princess Likelike had always dressed her daughter in much the same modes she herself favored —richly and modishly elaborate gowns of silks, satins, and velvets. While the gain in health made at Kona still benefited her pupil, Miss Gardinier approached the elder Princess with a suggestion that lighter clothing, better suited to a tropical climate, might prove beneficial.

To Kaiulani's surprise, Mama was not resentful and took the recommendation under consideration, with the result that, not long afterward, cooler and simpler dresses were provided. It was like a release from some imprisoning cocoon to feel so airy and free!

The year ended almost imperceptibly, except for the usual flurry at Christmas time. Suddenly the flowered calendar on Miss Gardinier's little table read 1886. January 16 was Mr. Gibson's sixty-second birthday, and this year as never before in Kaiulani's memory it was impressively celebrated at his big town house, Hale Aniani.

Hawaiians poured past his door all day, bearing tokens of respect and affection. Kaiulani herself was taken to the afternoon reception attended by royalty, members of the Cabinet, foreign diplomats—by everyone, in fact, except the clique of haole merchants and planters to whom Mr. Gibson represented an obstruction which must be destroyed.

Yet it was a strange sort of party, not at all the carefree fete to be expected of a birthday. Guests seemed to be rallying around the gaunt, crag-nosed old man as if around a battle standard. There was very little laughter. "Happy birthday!" people said. But it was not a happy occasion, though most of the guests had attended it out of love.

If any change was noticeable in life at Ainahau, as winter eased on toward spring, it was that the King came even less often than formerly on family calls. Serious government business held him in town. The seven-year-old Reciprocity Treaty between America and Hawaii had run its course; and now in distant Washington, where Mr. Grover Cleveland lately had taken over the duties of the President of the United States, a new treaty (so necessary to Hawaii's sugar prosperity) was being negotiated.

The United States was seeking exclusive rights to Pearl Harbor, a few miles out from the city, as a coaling and repair station for its Pacific ships. Native Hawaiians were raising a clamor against granting any foreign power such a concession. Americans, of course, applauded it.

On April 30, the new Legislature opened its sessions. Kaiulani knew that Papa Moi, angered by efforts of the self-styled "Reformers" to block every step of his government program, had campaigned personally for native candidates in the recent elections; and that, as a result, only ten "Reform" members had been elected. The *Gazette,* missionary-owned, screamed that voters had been bribed and fed gin and even threatened, in order to elect the King's candidates. The *Advertiser,* friendly to Papa Moi, answered them in kind.

Despite her occasional tempers, Kaiulani usually was a tractable child. But one afternoon, after the heat of summer had set in, she was still reveling in the cool water off Waikiki beach when Miss Gardinier called her in. For a length of time quite unlike her, Kaiulani ignored the summons. Finally she emerged, and sulked while her maids dressed her. Then, as she stepped out again into the sunlight, some devil took hold of her. Back into the water she raced, heedless of Miss Gardinier's cries and of the soaking of her pretty frock.

Her governess caught up with her. Miss Gardinier seized her by the shoulders, shook her, and administered a light slap of exasperation. Fury twisted Kaiulani's face as her first blank astonishment faded. She tore free and ran up the beach, shrilling, *"I'll tell my mother!"*

Miss Gardinier took the shortest way back to the gates of Ainahau, and from there to the garden cottage which was Princess Likelike's retreat. As the Princess listened to what had happened, a frown deepened between her eyes. It was obvious that she was deeply distressed. But not, Miss Gardinier promptly observed, because of her daughter's insubordination.

"You see, Miss Gardinier," she said, in chill reproof, "Kaiulani is a princess. And a princess cannot be punished."

Miss Gardinier stood her ground. "I'm very sorry, Your Highness, but a princess must learn to understand obedience, especially if it is for her own good. If she cannot be disciplined when necessary, then I cannot teach her. I herewith tender my resignation."

Old kapus and modern civilization did their battle in Likelike Cleghorn's still-frowning face before she answered stiffly.

"I wish to think this over, Miss Gardinier."

Miss Gardinier spent the remainder of the afternoon in her own quarters. Before dinner, she was summoned again to the cottage.

"Miss Gardinier," said Her Royal Highness, "I have been thinking it over, and I do not wish you to resign. Kaiulani was naughty and will apologize to you. I will decide upon some other method of discipline."

"No apology is necessary, Your Highness," Miss Gardinier replied. "But I should like time to consider withdrawing my resignation."

She had been back in her room only a brief while when a knock came at her door. Kaiulani walked in slowly, her dark eyes unhappy.

She spoke without prompting. "Miss Gardinier, I realize I was disobedient this afternoon, and I am very sorry."

"You see, Kaiulani," Miss Gardinier said, "there is something for *you* to think about. If you, as a princess, do not obey any authority, then how can you expect obedience from others?"

"I never thought of that," her young pupil admitted. "It was wrong. I'll never disobey you again." Now the delicate mouth quivered. "Mama said you might leave us. Oh, Miss *Gardinier!*" And she hurled herself across the shadowy room. *"Please* don't go away!"

"I will think about it, Kaiulani," Miss Gardinier promised. And next morning, after another serious talk with Princess Likelike in the garden cottage, she agreed to remain at Ainahau for another year.

Summer ran out and October arrived once more. A whole year since the gala birthday at Kaawaloa! In the Legislature, its president interrupted the bickerings between "Reformers" and Royalists to announce a communication from Her Royal Highness Princess Likelike and the Honorable Archibald S. Cleghorn, inviting the members and their ladies to a luau at one o'clock on Saturday, October 16, in honor of the eleventh birthday of their daughter.

Battle-weary lawmakers welcomed the excuse for a holiday

after their morning session, and by noon their carriages were thick along the road from the city. At Ainahau, a host and hostess never more gracious were waiting to receive them. In one of the spacious rooms, Kaiulani herself stood between guardian kahilis symbolic of her rank to accept their good wishes. Papa Moi, escorted by his chamberlain, arrived shortly after two o'clock. The rooms and gardens were filled with prominent personages.

The *Daily Bulletin* of the following Monday, describing the impressive event, said;

> Tables were literally loaded with national dishes, cooked in the ancient Hawaiian style of the culinary art. . . . A large side table was loaded with foreign food for the benefit of foreign guests not initiated in the ways of Hawaiian tables. . . . Provisions . . . were on the grand scale both as to quality and quantity. . . .

When the feasting ended, Papa Moi came to his feet. "Ladies and gentlemen," he said, with a courtly bow toward his sister's small daughter, "I arise to propose the health of Her Royal Highness Princess Kaiulani. On this occasion I am proud to pay this compliment to my niece as being a member of the direct line. I hope that she will grow up with all the advantages of the period, so that she may fill her position in the future to the credit of the nation."

This graceful speech was responded to, at the King's request, by the Honorable Sam Wilder: "May she indeed live to be the 'Hope of the Nation.' May her education be . . . such that when, in the natural events of life, she may rule over this land, may it be a rule of wisdom, always retaining the love of her people. Surely all here will say with me '*Aloha nui*' to the Princess Kaiulani."

In one large room, the gifts which had been arriving for Kaiulani were on display. So many presents of cash had poured in that Mama had appointed an official treasurer for the occasion to keep track of them all. There seemed no end to the offerings piled on the long tables. Among them, along with an album of ferns, was a birthday poem from Mr. L. Montgomery Mather, neatly engrossed upon a gilded card.

TO HER ROYAL HIGHNESS PRINCESS KAIULANI

Dear little Princess, joy to thee this day
That adds another year to thy young life,
Now bursting forth as tender buds in May,
To bloom, we pray, a stranger unto strife.

All that is sweet in life's springtime be thine.
Lose not an hour of youthful days too few;
Their happy memories will in future shine,
And bring to serious age a brighter hue.

Thus may thy course of life go gently on,
As each new year its beauties shall disclose,
And when the blush of summertime has gone,
Remaining years be full of sweet repose.

It had indeed been a brilliant if exhausting celebration, Kaiulani admitted at its close. Yet, in some way difficult to name, she felt in it a difference from the more spontaneous celebration at Kaawaloa the year before.

Today's luau had carried an almost official air. Would so many important Island personalities ever have gathered in one place, unless—unless what? Did this show of loyalty to the royal family have something to do with troubles Papa Moi was facing in his government? Had it all been arranged to impress upon doubters the firmness of the base upon which the Monarchy rested? But that would have been an odd use to make of a little girl's birthday, surely!

Almost more important than the birthday was another event which dominated that October. Miss Gardinier was engaged to be married!

Her fiancé was Mr. Albert W. Heydtmann, and (until this devastating crisis) he had seemed to Kaiulani one of the nicest of the young men who escorted her governess to balls and receptions. But now—although the wedding plans were not yet to be announced, because of Miss Gardinier's promise to stay on at Ainahau another year—Kaiulani took a different view.

An impressive framed photograph of Mr. Heydtmann appeared

in the place of honor on Miss Gardinier's bureau. Smiling there, it became for her pupil the symbol of all betrayals the world could hold.

One afternoon, soon after the advent of that hated picture, she was in Miss Gardinier's room after lessons. Slowly she walked over to the bureau and stood before it, studying every feature of the Enemy. Without warning, she lifted one hand and drew a thumbnail across Mr. Heydtmann's face, leaving a jagged scratch.

Later, of course, she apologized. It had been a shameful thing to do. But she had no apologies for the feeling that had inspired her naughtiness. A few afternoons later, Mr. Heydtmann called in person. Without preamble, Kaiulani walked up to him and spoke.

"Mr. Heydtmann, I hate you."

"Why, Princess Kaiulani!" Miss Gardinier's visitor obviously was unnerved. "What have I ever done to make you say that?"

"You are going to take Miss Gardinier away." Her eyes were bright with accusation. "She came out here to Hawaii for *me,* not for you." The obvious truth of her reproof, however, seemed entirely lost upon him. He did not offer to restore what he had stolen.

On November 16, a month to the day after her own luau, Papa Moi became fifty years old. The Legislature, dominated in its present session by loyal men, took time out from wrangling to declare a fitting celebration. A seven-day national holiday was proclaimed.

It began with a reception at Iolani Palace at which any Hawaiian, rich or poor, might bow before Their Majesties and offer his gift. There was a notable absence of members of the "Downtown Party." But diplomats and other members of the foreign colony crowded the impressive state rooms. Mormon children from Laie, on the other side of the island, were decked in ribbons lettered *Birthday of Our Beloved David.* In Honolulu, a monster torchlight parade put on by the Fire Department honored the King. Races and regattas and sporting events were brilliantly climaxed by a palace ball. The Reformers howled in their *Gazette.* But the Hawaiians paid little heed. They were well accustomed to being told that most things which brought no profit to the haoles were "outrages."

When events had ended in a state dinner, old Mr. Gibson attended a Hawaiian service at Kaumakapili Church and explained the celebration to the native congregation as a symbol of their national identity.

"You must be prepared for a changing future," he warned them. "You must advance. But do so as Polynesians!"

Kaiulani found reports of what he had said most engrossing. For now it had been put into words that birthdays—*some* birthdays—were not private possessions but public symbols. She could look back upon her own recent birthday, upon Papa Moi's and that of Mr. Gibson, in a new light. Having one's birthday become a "symbol" was a strange, sad milestone along the road to growing up.

6: Mama, Good-by

A shadow darkened the anticipated gaieties of the Christmas of 1886. Mama—always so vivacious that she seemed to shimmer like light on water—grew unaccountably quiet and retired to her bed, stubbornly refusing to eat her meals. Social activity at Ainahau slowed to a round of sickroom callers.

There were whispers. Superstitious servants of the household were heard to murmur that Mama was being prayed to death by a *kahuna,* one of those fearsome old men who, in ancient days before the missionaries came, had been believed to possess supernatural powers.

Of course, any good Christian knew there was no such thing as evil magic. But even more, the stories were disproved by the very fact that the victim of the hinted "spells" was Mama. No native in the Island failed to love and revere her. Even what might be considered to be Mama's faults—her swift rages, her frequently arrogant pride—were qualities the Hawaiians looked for and admired in their alii, their hereditary leaders. The notion any one of them might wish her harm was absurd.

Still, the big house settled to an unnatural silence. Doctors made daily visits, the creak of their carriage wheels becoming familiar on the drive. Papa confided in Kaiulani that plans were being made to send both Mama and herself to California in April, as soon as the physicians would permit their patient to travel.

45

As January ended, friends visiting the invalid were full of talk about the departure for Samoa of a Hawaiian legation to solicit an alliance with King Malietoa of that other Polynesian kingdom. Papa Moi anticipated forming a league of Pacific Island kingdoms, with himself at its head. United, they might hope to stem the greed for territories growing more evident in various European powers and the United States.

Callers at Ainahau buzzed with such reports. But to Kaiulani, the violent outbreak of the volcano Mauna Loa was more dramatic news. Fire burst from the molten heart of Hawaii's great mountain on January 16, and within two days a major eruption was under way on the Big Island. The flow of lava was said to be moving with unprecedented speed, wiping out roads and farms in its path. Natives who fled before it brought reports that a great school of red *akule* fish (whose appearance traditionally foretold the death of a high chief) had been sighted in the waters off Kau. No one with Hawaiian blood in his veins could have suppressed entirely the fear that threatened to engulf Kaiulani's common sense. Generations of her mother's people had believed in the vengeful powers of the volcano goddess Pele and her fires. And the arrival of the dread akule had been accepted since earliest history as an omen of disaster.

The doctors had informed Papa that they could find nothing wrong with Mama physically—nothing except the acute exhaustion induced by her continued refusal to take nourishment. If only she might be persuaded to *try!* During her bedside visits, Kaiulani earnestly set herself to discussing topics that might strike some spark of interest.

There were, for example, the stained-glass windows that each of the princesses was donating to the new cathedral at St. Andrew's. Designs were now being made. Princess Likelike had chosen the Resurrection as the subject for her gift; and surely (thought her small daughter, whose own window would depict Joseph taken from the pit) a note of hope should be struck from such a subject. Yet, in dismay, Kaiulani sensed that Mama did not expect to live until her window was ready.

When the day actually came, Kaiulani was not prepared for

it. The second of February. She was at her morning lessons when word was brought that she was wanted in the sickroom. When she came out of it, a good while later, she was weeping heart-brokenly. She flung herself into the dependable arms of her governess.

"Oh, Miss Gardinier, my mother is dying! And she told me she could see my future very plainly. I am to go far away for a long time, I will never marry, and I will never be queen!"

Sympathetic fingers stroked her bent head. "Now then, now then! Very often, when people are as ill as Her Highness, they believe they see things in the future. But it's only part of their illness."

"But if Mama is dying, if she isn't going to be here any more—"

"Then you'll have to be as brave as you know how, and live your life as best you possibly can. But we mustn't give up hoping, Kaiulani."

Carriages came and went through the gates marked "Kapu." The King and Aunt Liliu arrived from Honolulu, to be taken to the room where Mama lay. They remained there behind closed doors for a considerable time. The two family physicians were in constant attendance, aided now by two others who had been hastily summoned. But there never really had been any doubt of what was about to happen. At a little after four o'clock in the afternoon, they came from the silent house with a gravity which told its own story.

Looking ill himself and suddenly a dozen years older, Papa asked Miss Gardinier to receive the callers who inevitably would come. Then he and Kaiulani retired to their private rooms, each to find a personal armor behind which grief could hide. The creak of wheels below the windows became almost a steady sound as night drew on.

As the moon rose, the grieving kanakas who had loved her best began to gather in their lost Likelike's gardens. They came softly, tears on their faces. But long before midnight, when custom decreed the start of the procession conveying Her Highness to the palace where she would lie in state, the wailing for the dead had begun. Eerie and heartbroken, it lifted and diminished and lifted again. In days as recent as those of Aunt Liliu's girlhood, subjects had knocked out their teeth and tattooed their tongues and shaved their heads when an alii died. The few intervening decades had not wiped out entirely those ancient manifestations of grief. Plaintive and piercing, the wails reached Kaiulani's bedroom.

Papa had invited Miss Gardinier to join the sad procession when it left Ainahau for the city. Slowly, a line of carriages and of simpler folk afoot made its way along the townward miles Likelike had so often driven in vivacious happiness. The King and Queen and Aunt Liliu had come to escort the body of their younger sister on its way, and Kaiulani huddled in a Cleghorn carriage at Papa's side.

As protocol required, she was to remain in residence at the palace (together with the other alii of Mama's rank) until the day of the funeral, three weeks later. That first night, or what remained of it, seemed to Kaiulani to endure forever. She would have given much for the comfort of Miss Gardinier's arms. But her beloved governess already had returned to Waikiki. Kaiulani felt more alone than anyone in the world.

The first of the official observances for a dead princess was a requiem service held in the throne room at ten o'clock next morning. The Bishop of Honolulu presided, assisted by the Reverend Alexander MacIntosh. Only the family attended. At the conclusion of the ritual, the palace gates were opened and the throngs who had gathered in the streets outside began to file in endless line—hour after hour—past the catafalque at the center of the throne room.

Mama lay there in a robe of purest white satin, the Orders of Kalakaua and Kamehameha pinned to her breast, her face calm and still and—whenever Kaiulani braced herself to look upon it—frighteningly like the face of a stranger. Around the bier ranged the tireless kahili bearers, and a detachment of officers from the Household Guard, all standing like statues. Flowers massed on tables and stands all about the room filled the hot afternoon with their heavy sweetness. At the foot of the bier stood a cross, emblem of Christianity; and at its head, on crimson cushions, were displayed Mama's coronet and other Orders.

Throughout the three weeks of ceremonies, the palace was home to Kaiulani. But every afternoon Miss Gardinier drove in from Waikiki to bring her comfort and companionship, to read aloud to her, to walk with her through Iolani's handsome park. Those visits brought the only touch of familiarity to strange days. Always before so exciting, the palace seemed now to Kaiulani like a prison.

After Mama's removal from Ainahau, the thousands of gardenias brought there by friends who remembered they were her favorite flower had been burned. The perfume of them, Kaiulani was told, had lingered over the district for days. And afterward she was to remember this report frequently, for it was true that gardenias failed to bloom in Oahu gardens for several years after Mama's funeral, and particularly at Waikiki.

At first, the public feeling about Mama's death seemed entirely of respect and sympathy. A writer in the *Hawaiian Gazette* grew unashamedly sentimental while describing

the young chiefess' first ball. It was at the old Court House, on the occasion of an entertainment given by the staff officers to Kamehameha V. It was a slight girlish figure, simply clad in white, with a fragrant wreath of flowers twisted in the glossy black hair—so bright and merry was the face. And a few days ago one gazed upon the same face and figure, grown almost girlish again in that "First dark day of nothingness, The last of danger and distress." . . .

Then, gradually, as the days passed, an ugly note crept in. Half-rumors vaguely recognized at Ainahau rose louder here, at the heart of the city. And there were fewer devoted attendants to keep them from Kaiulani's ears. What she heard left her shaken as if by a physical fever.

The kahuna who was supposed to have prayed the late Princess into eternal darkness, these sly innuendoes hinted, was none other than David Kalakaua himself. It was well known, the whispers intimated, that His Majesty had prayed Queen Emma to death as punishment for her political opposition. Now he had sacrificed a member of his own family to the pagan gods of ancient Hawaii, in an effort to reaffirm through their favor his grip on his kingdom. And this, it was said, had been done with the blessing of Princess Liliuokalani, jealous of the double threat of Likelike and Kaiulani to her own inheritance of the throne.

The obvious absurdities in the rumors seemed to do little to check their malicious circulation. Everyone knew that Aunt Liliu, her life long devoted to Mama and of rigidly Christian character, had been legal heir to the throne for a decade and had no cause for "jealousy." Everyone knew that his gay younger sister had been the darling of Papa Moi's eye. Still, the ugly stories would not be hushed. Mama's admittedly mysterious loss of the will to live was seized upon as proof.

For the first time in her life, Kaiulani stood face to face with real evil; evil deliberate and purposeful, even though those who perpetrated it were without faces or names. The King and Aunt Liliu had suffered enough without this slander! In her anger, Kaiulani experienced a new first-hand knowledge of the struggle that had gone on so long between the throne of Hawaii and men intent upon destroying it.

The day of the royal funeral dawned at last—February 23, a Sunday. At half-past nine precisely, morning prayers were read for a last time in the throne room. Some hundred and fifty of the city's most prominent citizens were gathered for the service. Kaiulani stood small and rigid at the head of the coffin, with Papa on one side and Papa Moi on the other, while the Reverend Mr. MacIntosh officiated.

The funeral itself began on the stroke of one o'clock. Invitations had been issued only to officials and diplomats, yet the hall was filled. On the raised throne dais, draped in black through which the crimson of its customary hangings burned dimly like a banked fire, sat the King and Queen, Aunt Liliu, and Princess Poomaikalani. Still at the center of the room was the coffin, draped in a heavy black pall worked for it by the sisters of St. Andrew's Priory and lined with white satin and embroidered with the monogram K.L., for Kapili Likelike. Sixteen kahili bearers, in double row, kept up that rhythmic waving of feathered standards which had not halted since the arrival of Mama's body from Ainahau. After the organist had played an *"In Memoriam"* march which he had composed especially for the somber occasion, the Bishop and clergy took their places.

"I am the Resurrection and the Life saith the Lord. . . ."

Kaiulani kept her eyes lowered. To gaze along the rows of reverent faces would be to seek behind each one; to guess which faces masked the men who had spread such poison about the family of a princess to whom they now paid surface homage. She dared not think, either, about Mama. All these weeks, while she had done her duty as part of the official pageant of mourning, she had not dared really to think about Mama. "The Lord giveth and the Lord taketh away; blessed be the name of the Lord. . . ."

To Handel's Death March in *Saul,* the congregation dispersed slowly, flowing through the outer corridor and down the wide palace steps. Twelve stalwart policemen shouldered the heavy coffin and bore it down to the catafalque drawn up in waiting at the bottom step. Far off across the city, minute guns of the battery on Punchbowl Hill boomed news of the start of Mama's last journey. For two hours, the time required for the procession, the guns would sound each minute like some clock of doom.

Drawn by lines of reverent Hawaiians pulling twin ropes covered with black and white ribbons, the catafalque began to roll. Black plumes nodded and the gilt crown on the dome quivered with the bier's motion. The coffin of shining *koa* and *kau* woods gleamed with Mama's own enameled crest and motto: *E hii i ke Kapu* ("The Sacred One will be held in the protecting arms").

With Papa still at her side and lost in rememberings of his own, Kaiulani endured the two hours from palace to mausoleum gates. The Cleghorn carriage was first in line, with other mourners directly behind it and a long line of Hawaiians following afoot. The big Punchbowl guns kept booming, their thunder shivering back off the mountains.

At the mausoleum, as soon as the coffin had been placed in its crypt, the Bishop intoned the remainder of the Episcopal burial service. An Hawaiian choir, tears on their coppery faces, first chanted the Twenty-Second Psalm and then raised their voices in the hymn "Now the Laborer's Task Is O'er." And then the ordeal was over.

Back down the valley the Cleghorn carriage rolled, along streets from which the crowds already had dispersed. Mama lay asleep forever. At Ainahau (no matter how often one would come into a room and feel that she must only now have left it by some other door) there could be no more of her gala parties, no more of her fashionable dresses arriving from California, no more of her sudden violent tempers and equally sudden sunshine.

Now that no one was watching, it was safe at last to think about Mama. To remember things it was good to remember. Like that way she'd had of hiding *pikake* in the black coils of her hair, so that one could not see the blossoms yet never lost the whisper of a fragrance as she passed.

7: At Bayonet's Point

The weeks went by quietly. Miss Gardinier had been persuaded to stay on at Ainahau until the very day of her May wedding. Lessons and daily walks and long discussions filled the slow time.

In the newspapers brought out from the city, references to Mama had taken a legal turn. Said the *Gazette,* a week after the funeral: "A document purporting to be the will of the late Princess Miriam Likelike Cleghorn was filed in the Supreme Court. . . . The only devisee mentioned in the will is her daughter, the Princess Kaiulani. . . ." And a short time later: "The Hon. A. S. Cleghorn has been appointed by Mr. Justice Preston trustee under the will of the late Princess Likelike. . . ."

But far more interesting was news of the King's decision to send Mama Moi and a retinue (including Aunt Liliu and Uncle John Dominis) to London. There they were to represent Hawaii among the crowned heads of the world at Queen Victoria's much-heralded Golden Jubilee. The suite and their servants were booked aboard the outgoing *Australia* for April 12. A flurry of preparation spread ripples even as far as Ainahau, as Kaiulani pestered Miss Gardinier with an avalanche of questions about the states and cities through which her aunts and their party would pass.

Her British Majesty's Ship *Caroline* reached port only a few days after the Queen's departure; and Kalakaua thought it proper to issue invitations to a dance honoring her officers, headed by

Captain Sir William Wiseman. For this event, which signaled the end of the period of official mourning for Mama, the palace bloomed with flowers and bunting. But the feature of the evening which caused audible gasps of wonder was the illumination of the entire grounds—not merely the palace interior, as heretofore —with its new electric lights. Crowds passed the fences all evening to marvel at this latest magic of science and the company upon whom it shone.

Now Kaiulani steeled herself to face yet another loss. The date of Miss Gardinier's marriage to Mr. Heydtmann had been set months before for May 10. Until Mama's death, it had been planned that the reception following the ceremony would be held at Ainahau. Although this affectionate intention could not be carried out, the wedding itself was to take place in St. Andrew's Cathedral at eight in the evening.

Miss Gardinier had remained on duty almost until the last possible moment. At four o'clock on the day of the wedding, Kaiulani walked out with her to the carriage Papa had ordered. She had to concentrate fiercely on holding back her tears, as she saw it move away down the shade-dappled driveway.

A few hours later, at Papa's side, she was among the large and distinguished group who gathered at the Cathedral to hear the Reverend Mr. Wallace read the marriage service. The King occupied the front pew and a shining Miss Gardinier came down the aisle on the arm of American Minister-Resident Merrill to meet a pale but obviously devoted bridegroom before the altar. A scent of flowers hung sweet on the May evening and the music lifted—and oh, it would have been wicked to have begrudged these two their happiness!

Scraps of news were soon drifting back to Honolulu from the royal travelers. They had been received with formal salutes at the Golden Gate and shown every honor in their progress across the United States.

Dutifully (and a bit wistfully) Kaiulani wrote to the Queen.

My dear Aunt:

   . . . I hope that you will enjoy your trip to Washington, I would like to be with you very much. I received a very nice letter from Kawananakoa and one from Kuhio telling me that they went over to San Francisco to meet you, and that you went over to see the school at San Mateo. . . .

Papa has got the position of Collector General of Customs, because Kapena is put out. . . .

This business of Papa's appointment still somewhat bewildered her. What turn in politics had been responsible for veteran Mr. Kapena's replacement she did not truly comprehend. But on the last morning of April the King had sent for Papa to offer him the post. As it was the first time Mama's royal brother had offered his relative-by-marriage any office by his personal appointment, Papa had thought it wise to accept.

News from America continued to be exciting. A formal dinner had been given for the royal visitors to Washington by President Cleveland and his popular First Lady. Boston, as well, greeted them handsomely. And Queen Victoria herself had cabled that the travelers were to be her personal guests while in London. In view of such honors for Hawaii, it was difficult to explain why the haoles in their *Gazette* protested the journey as "a robbery of public funds."

Papa had engaged a new governess to take (nominally, at least) Miss Gardinier's place. A Frenchwoman this time, whose name was Miss D'Alcala, she took up residence at Ainahau during the later weeks of May. On the black-bordered stationery she and Papa had used since Mama's death, Kaiulani wrote to Aunt Liliu, now in London, "I like her very much, she is nice but a little strict. . . ."

Edward Keliiahoui and Jonah Kuhio, the younger two of the Queen's three nephews, came home on vacation from their military school at San Mateo, California, and for a brief while boisterous young male laughter rang again in Ainahau's gardens. Happily receiving her princely "cousins," Kaiulani thought often of the eldest of the trio—handsome David Kawananakoa. "Koa" was now all but a man grown, and had gone east at the same time as his royal aunt, to begin schooling at King's College in England.

Throughout the latter half of the spring, haole newspapers had been intensifying their attacks upon Mr. Gibson and the King. The government had recently granted its license to import opium to a wealthy Chinese merchant, Chun Lung, who had paid eighty thousand dollars for the franchise. Now the hostile *Gazette* published a "confession" by another Chinese, Aki, who claimed that Kalakaua personally had accepted a large bribe from him for the same license already sold to Chun.

The business clique made an uproar about the King's "dishonesty." But Mr. Gibson turned up positive evidence that the "confession" had been notarized in the office of lawyers representing enemies of the Crown; and that Aki could not read, and hence did not know what he signed. Headlines and gossip swept over the city like lava from an eruption.

An anti-royalist organization calling itself the Hawaiian League had been formed in the city. And those concerned for the government were greatly worried by the activities of a self-styled Committee of Thirteen. On the last night in June, the League held a great rally at the armory on Beretania Street to whip up "popular indignation."

Only a handful of Hawaiian faces were to be seen among the crowd of idly curious Asiatics and whites. A well-drilled claque applauded wildly every attack made upon the King by inflammatory orators. It booed to silence the common-sense remarks of moderate citizens.

A delegation marched from the armory to the palace to present the rally's demands: dismissal of Mr. Gibson, appointment of a new Cabinet pleasing to the rebels, and the drafting of a new constitution. The regime to be established would greatly weaken the throne. It put government in the hands of only those residents meeting a property qualification set high enough to disenfranchise most native Hawaiians. It made the voting class the haole foreigners, not even citizens of Hawaii.

The Committee of Thirteen was able to enforce its demands because its members previously had gathered most of the firearms in Honolulu, under the pretext that they were to be used in Rifle Club drills. Even a major portion of Papa Moi's own palace armament had been secretly purloined, and he stood virtually defenseless at bayonet point.

Essentially a mob, the rebels behaved with a mob's fury. Mr. Gibson and his son-in-law, Mr. Hayselden, were dragged from their homes with nooses about their necks. They would have been lynched, except that British Consul Waterhouse threatened to turn the guns of a British warship anchored in harbor against the city unless the prisoners were released. This brought grudging order to the crowd. Mr. Gibson was held under guard until a departing steamer could exile him from the Islands.

The week's dramatic events were not all perfectly understood by Kaiulani in the quiet gardens out at Ainahau. Although she knew that troubles of some nature were afoot, her uncle was so affectionate and serene when she was taken to pay a call on him at the palace that she could only assume the overheard gossip was exaggerated. She wrote to Mama Moi almost as if nothing unusual were happening.

> I went to see Papa Moi and he told me you would soon be home so I will not write much. . . . My new governess is with me now, and I have to study many things so I am busy all day. . . . The boys return to school tomorrow and I am very sorry they must go before your return. I will only have to wait a few days now before I have you all back with me. . . .

If one were to believe the surface signs, peace and amity had been restored to the tiny kingdom. It was possible for Kaiulani to put aside her anxieties and take pleasure in the fact that, a few days later, Papa was appointed acting governor of Oahu to serve until Uncle John Dominis returned to assume his duties.

On August 2, Mama Moi and her suite returned from their triumphs abroad to a sadly altered Hawaii. Papa and Kaiulani were in the party aboard the little steam tug *Eleu* when it put out to meet the arriving *Australia.* All the vessels in harbor were breaking out gala bunting as the *Eleu* bobbed past. Aquiver with anticipation, Kaiulani sat near the tug's bow; and as it began to circle the stately *Australia,* she waved with a frenzy that Papa doubtless considered most unladylike.

At the Inter-Island Wharf a gathering of dignitaries waited. From the tear-streaked yet smiling faces lining the Queen's route to the palace, from the heartfelt cries of *"Aloha,"* one could not have guessed what evil times the rulers of Hawaii had come upon. Or perhaps one could. For almost without exception the faces were Polynesian, the faces of a people cheated, outraged, and helpless when their Moi was humbled.

In the days that followed, life tended to settle into at least an imitation of its old routines. Uncle John Dominis resumed his post as governor of Oahu, and Papa stepped down. At Ainahau, Miss D'Alcala's brief term as Kaiulani's governess ended and she was replaced by a German, Miss Reiseberg. But Kaiulani was learning to accept change.

The hardest change of all to accept was death. Although Mama was gone, and Miss Barnes, and old Princess Ruth, and others she had known since childhood, her own green generation had not been invaded until now.

But in September her lifelong playmate Edward—so recently on vacation and racing through the gardens—arrived home suddenly from school in San Mateo, the victim of a relapse after scarlet fever. He was taken directly from his ship to the palace on a Tuesday, and the very next afternoon word was abroad in the city that he had died. "Prince Edward Abel Keliiahoui . . . adopted and brought up by H.R.H. Princess Poomaikalani . . . nephew to Queen Kapiolani. . . ." All the facts were in the news, correctly spelled out. But—*Edward?* Only eighteen years old?

Almost a young lady now, Kaiulani found herself taking an increased part in the events with which autumn began. Appreciation of the royal family did seem to continue. Early in November, the *Gazette* reported discovery (in a box of goods shipped to the newspaper) of two informal scraps of paper from California. On one was scribbled "Your Queen is a dandy," and on the other, more circumspectly, "I had the pleasure of seeing your Queen. L. Duffy." Crumbs, perhaps. But hurt pride can feed on crumbs.

Papa Moi's fifty-first birthday was officially celebrated with a big regatta to which native crowds and even many haole sport-lovers thronged despite a constantly falling rain. The shimmering curtain dropping from the clouds seemed like tears for Hawaii, shed by her old gods.

There was much to be wept over. The Reformers were busier now snatching their own dirty linen from public view than they had been at cleaning up the old "abuses." A farce trial of poor ex-Premier Gibson was conducted *in absentia.* But the public recognized whitewash where they saw it, and were not fooled. Every juror in the box had been a member of those Rifles whose bayonets had backed up the revolution.

Whatever troubles the Reformers might be having with public approval, they met none at all with their iron control of the government. The King had been compelled by them to announce an extension for seven years of the Reciprocity Treaty with their homeland—to which had been added a clause which granted "to national vessels of the United States the exclusive privilege of entering Pearl Harbor and establishing there a coaling and repair station." How Papa Moi must have detested setting his signature to that concession! But so the year ended. And 1888 began.

The new year was not a month old when word reached Honolulu of the death in California hospital of the Reformers' archenemy, Mr. Gibson. In mid-February, the S.S. *Zealandia* arrived in port bearing the austere black casket with solid gold handles in which the body reposed. By the tens of thousands, Hawaiians lined the streets along which members of two native societies drew the catafalque from the waterfront to serene old Hale Aniani, where their one-time defender would lie in state. Many a Reformer must be sighing in relief, Kaiulani thought, because their old foe never again could rise to oppose them. But on the afternoon she herself was brought in from Ainahau to pay her respects, the music room of the old house was filled with weeping natives who mourned a friend.

It was perplexing how such a time of darkness could also be a time of progress. On March 23, for the first time, all Honolulu was lit by electricity. Punctually at seven in the evening, the Reformers' Minister of the Interior—Mr. Lorrin Thurston—escorted Kaiulani and Aunt Liliu into the gleamingly clean electric light station up the valley. Here they were greeted by the superintendent and his assistant, each in work garb including a cap that resembled a crow at rest on a barn. A chair was brought for Kaiulani to stand on; and, with the superintendent to guide her hand, she threw the switch which connected the circuits to illuminate the city in a sudden blaze like daylight. For such innovations, one had to grant the Reformers a share of the credit.

Yet many of the recent "outstanding achievements" to which the new regime pointed with pride were not really their own doing—for example, the new railway being constructed by Mr. Benjamin Dillingham, who never had been one of them. He had defeated their efforts to wrest control of his ambitious project from him, and now had track stretching well toward the Ewa district—in spite of (and not because of) the Reformers!

October brought with it Kaiulani's thirteenth birthday. And on the last day of the year the Queen's fifty-third birthday was observed. On both occasions the native Hawaiians displayed their abiding love for their highest alii. Kaiulani's was marked by a reception at Ainahau almost as impressive as any of Mama's day. And Kapiolani's was celebrated by a royal salute from the shore battery and a general displaying of flags.

From eleven in the morning until two in the afternoon, Mama Moi held a state reception for ladies at Iolani Palace. What seemed an unending line of callers filed past Her Majesty where she received them in the throne room, impressively attired in the beautiful court gown of peacock feathers made for her to wear at Queen Victoria's Jubilee. Aunt Liliu was there with her lady-in-waiting, Mrs. Aldrich; and Kaiulani was attended by Annie Cleghorn and her governess, Miss Reiseberg. Rosie Cleghorn's husband, Jim Robertson, acted as chamberlain for the King, ushering in the visitors to a Blue Room bowered in ferns and flowers.

Excitement unconnected with the birthday spread through the rooms when it was rumored that the yacht *Casco* had been sighted off Diamond Head. It already was known in Honolulu that the world-admired writer Robert Louis Stevenson—whose stepdaughter, Isobel Strong, was a popular member of the court circle and wife of the official court painter—was on his way to

Hawaii from travels through the South Seas. The ripple at the Queen's reception turned out to be premature, however. When the Strongs were rowed out to meet the incoming vessel, she proved to be the beautiful *Nyanza,* owned by another socially popular resident, Captain Dewar.

Not until Thursday, January 24, did the overdue *Casco* slide into harbor, to drop anchor in the stream off the Oceanic Steamship Company wharf. On the following evening the Dewars were giving an "at home" aboard their *Nyanza.* The canopy over the yacht's decks was made of the flags of all the nations represented in the Islands.

Rowing out from the landing with Papa in the yacht's gig, Kaiulani gazed eagerly ahead toward a fairyland of lanterns strung all along the *Nyanza's* sides and from her prodigious seventy-foot boom. On a deck lit with massed lamps in banks of greenery, a throng of guests promenaded in evening dress or naval uniforms. Overhead, the yacht's twelve thousand yards of canvas hung furled against a higher dome of stars.

A piano had been brought up on deck, and all through the evening the musical talents of the guests were put to good use. With one of the Widemann girls, Annie Cleghorn sang "The Gypsy Countess." Kaiulani herself joined them in a ukelele trio. Lieut. Clark of the *Conquest* sang in a powerful baritone to the accompaniment of his own guitar.

Across a light-splattered harbor the *Casco* could be seen riding peacefully as if she slept after a long buffeting on the seas. It was too dark to make out anyone aboard her. But Kaiulani could imagine the people there. Robert Louis Stevenson, right here in Honolulu! A genuine literary celebrity!

8: Tusitala

"Tusitala," they had called the famous writer in Tahiti. The word meant "teller of tales," and was often used to describe him by those Kaiulani heard discussing the whirl of social events which followed his arrival. Settled into the Waikiki beach cottage of Mr. Henry Poor—a cottage called "Manuia," the Samoan word for "Welcome"—Mr. Stevenson called at the palace to pay his respects to Papa Moi. Almost immediately, Kalakaua returned the call aboard the *Casco*.

Next, Henry Poor issued invitations to a luau in honor of his celebrated friend. No less interesting than the native dishes served was the company assembled to devour them. Papa Moi was at the head of the table, tall even when seated, handsome and imposing and proud. Matching his dignity, Maggie Stevenson—the author's mother—sat at the King's left, her starched white widow's cap exactly like those worn by another widow in far-away Windsor Castle. And on her brother's right, between him and Stevenson, sat Aunt Liliu, massive but graceful and witty.

Others lining the long eating mat included dark Isobel Strong, Stevenson's stepdaughter, and her fair mother, Fanny Stevenson; Jim Robertson, attending as the King's chamberlain; bespectacled young Mr. Lloyd Osborne, Fanny Stevenson's son. Native girls stood behind the King and the author, waving over them the ceremonial kahilis, while Stevenson and Papa Moi dipped poi from a handsome communal koa calabash.

Late in the evening, after many royal toasts, the guest of honor produced from his pocket a neat package which he presented to Kalakaua. Inside, the King discovered a golden pearl—and a poem Stevenson had written to accompany it, which described his offering as:

> . . . Now doubly precious, since it pleased a king.
> The right, my liege, is ancient as the lyre
> For bards to give to kings what kings admire;
> 'Tis mine to offer, for Apollo's sake,
> And since the gift is fitting, yours to take.
> To golden hands the golden pearl I bring,
> The ocean jewel to the Island King.

When Papa described this compliment to Kaiulani, she wondered what Mr. Stevenson might have thought if he had dined with a King of Hawaii only a few generations ago. For in those days, not so very far gone, a chief's calabash would have been ornamented with the teeth of his slain enemies. And the staffs of his kahilis would have been inlaid with the shinbones of defeated rival princes.

In the past, Honolulu had welcomed a fair share of travelers from the world beyond the sea, but in Kaiulani's brief lifetime none of Robert Louis Stevenson's illustrious reputation. For her his very name cast a spell. Thinking of him, she could forget something which of late had been troubling her deeply. It had recently been decided by Papa Moi—and consented to by Papa —that very soon now she herself was to be banished to a school beyond those same seas.

Presently the Stevensons moved from Manuia to the Frank Brown villa adjoining it. They had more space here, and a little cottage in the garden where Mr. Stevenson could work; for he was busy finishing a novel to be called *The Master of Ballantrae*. The move was also a health measure. Already the newcomers were a hub of social activity. Royalists and missionaries alike crowded to visit them, every artist and musician in the Islands, every officer off a foreign man-of-war, everyone who welcomed convivial companionship. Fanny Stevenson had begun to worry quite openly about the strain this steady flow of callers had placed upon her delicate husband. He needed a place to retreat to when he was tired.

Kaiulani was sitting under her banyan late one afternoon when she heard steps in the driveway. It was early for Papa to be returning from town, and she glanced up in surprise. The steps came closer, distinct across the racket of the peacocks, and then she saw him—a thin, exotic figure emerging from the tunnel of shade under the trees.

He was a tall man, although perhaps not matching Papa's height, and seemed taller because he was so painfully thin. Invalid pallor had left his rather long and sensitive face almost chalky in color. His hair was dark and worn long, in a style no resident of Honolulu—haole or native—had ever affected.

His costume was equally distinctive—white flannels, a velveteen jacket, a loose shirt, and a flowing tie. Papa Moi, so dapper in his uniforms and his tailor-made whites, would not have used it to adorn a palace scarecrow. Yet on this particular man the bizarre collection of garments seemed peculiarly right.

"Good afternoon," he said, in a soft and haunting voice. Illness had eaten greedily into his thin face. But his eyes were large and dark and they made her think of two burning stars. "Mr. Cleghorn did me the honor to suggest that I call. My name is—"

"I know," said Kaiulani eagerly. "You're Mr. Stevenson."

It was the first of many afternoons they spent together, the poet and the princess, in her banyan's shade. He was the easiest person to talk with she ever had known. She actually could confess to him her dread of leaving Hawaii, as she so soon must. Mr. Stevenson brought all his storytelling skill to bear upon the sympathetically assumed task of bringing England alive for her. And it was reassuring to discover that even world-renowned people like her new friend had their own problems.

The chief one for Mr. Stevenson seemed to be his lack of money. He eagerly awaited the arrival of each steamer's mailbag (which he spoke of as Pandora's Box) and its possible financial reinforcements. In addition to *The Master of Ballantrae,* of which Stevenson was at work upon a tenth magazine installment, he and his stepson Lloyd also were completing together a story to be called *The Wrong Box,* which they hoped would be sold for cash-in-hand to alleviate the family's monetary strain. Stevenson told her jokingly that if a remittance from America did not arrive soon, he would apply to her uncle, the King, for work as his palace doorkeeper.

Young though she was, Kaiulani had assumed the formal duties of hostess at Ainahau and struggled to carry them out as Mama would have done. If her distinguished friend remembered her with some small gift, as not infrequently he did, her reply would be graciously immediate.

Mr. Stevenson: Dear Sir:
Your kind note has come. I thank you for it. Papa and I would like to have you come to our house on Tuesday next for dinner and Papa promises good Scotch "kaukau" for all you folks.
My pony Fairie has a cold today so I cannot go riding. When you come please bring with you your flute.
I am your most affectionate and obedient friend.
                                                                Kaiulani C.

To such invitations, prompt acknowledgement would be forth-coming:

Dearest Child:
I do most heartily welcome the opportunity to dine with you and your respected father on the evening of Tuesday, the 23 inst. I hope you have found time to read through the book which I have given you.
                                                                Most respectfully,
                                                                Robert L. Stevenson

After one of her afternoon swims, Kaiulani might discover that the governess waiting for her under a *hau* tree was no longer alone. Mr. Stevenson would stand there with her, fanning himself slowly.

"I've been pleading my case with your duenna, Kaiulani," he might say. "She agrees—but none too willingly, mind—that I may take you off to call on my family. I'm to return you to your father's house."

So, unexpectedly, she would find herself crossing the curving scimitar of sand with her thin, oddly clad friend beside her.

As they strolled along, he might report to her on the activities of a small mouse with whom he had made friends. Soon after he had begun working in his tiny cabin under the oleanders, this previous occupant had presented himself with pert timidity— terrified, yet irresistibly drawn by the aromas of the breakfast trays fetched to the workshop for his early-rising employer by the family's Chinese cook, Ah Fu.

Mr. Stevenson often tootled serenades to the mouse on his flageolet. Also, he made it a custom to save choice scraps from his simple meals. After a few mornings, the mouse had come down quite fearlessly off the high shelf from which it had watched. And so they had been friends ever since.

When they reached the edge of the Brown property, Kaiulani and her escort could see the main house with its big lanai flung open to the gardens, and beyond it a ramshackle building that was a combination kitchen, storeroom, and studio. The studio was hedged, usually, with the canvases painted by Mrs. Strong's husband, court artist Joseph Strong.

The wide lanai was, like most typical Hawaiian verandas, open on three sides to catch the breeze. On evenings already becoming legendary in Honolulu, lamps would burn late on all the little tables. But in the afternoon, sunlight shimmered through the trees to spill a radiance over the South Seas curiosities the Stevensons had collected during their travels—war clubs, idols, stone axes, shells.

On the lanai the family would await them. Kaiulani's first graceful curtsey was always for the senior Mrs. Stevenson, who generally sat stitching on a *kapa*, a traditional Hawaiian quilt. Again the curtsey, this time to Fanny Osborne Stevenson, almost a beauty in her way, who would reply with a gracious nod that set her favorite shoulder-brushing half-moon earrings to swaying. And after the younger Mrs. Stevenson, to her daughter. Mrs. Strong had been Mama's dear friend. The dark, dramatic-looking young woman always had some greeting to call back those happier days.

Mrs. Strong's younger brother, Lloyd Osborne, was a thin six-footer who appeared to be an odd combination of scholar and pirate. The contrast between his professorial spectacles and the tiny gold rings flashing in his earlobes was more than a trifle confusing.

As such an afternoon lengthened, Mr. Stevenson might play for them a spirited tune on the flageolet which entertained the mouse. Lloyd Osborne might accompany his music on the guitar. Everyone enjoyed the impromptu concerts, but Mr. Stevenson himself seemed to be having the finest time of all. He openly reveled in his new-found health. "After so many years, to find myself sea-bathing and cutting about like a grown-up person! I'll be sorry to leave, and that's the truth. But soon my mother must return to Edinburgh. Then Fanny, Lloyd, and I plan to push on again, for another year perhaps, among other islands."

Time passed so pleasantly that Kaiulani was always surprised to find the light lying long across the off-shore reef. Regretfully, she would murmur farewells to the others and—with Mr. Stevenson once more beside her—walk across the green lawns toward the road.

They must pass through a gate in the palings, where a big tub held darting goldfish, and veer toward nearby Ainahau. Afternoon would have cooled to a mellow stillness. Ahead, up the curving Cleghorn driveway, her peacocks would be screaming their familiar, unlovely tirades until the green shade seemed to quiver with their cries. And here—for a day or two, at least—she would take reluctant leave of her friend Tusitala.

9: Forth from Her Land

And now only a handful of time was left before the day she had been dreading. A public announcement of it already had appeared in the *Advertiser:*

> Princess Kaiulani will leave for England in May, in charge of Mrs. T. R. Walker, and will be accompanied by Miss Annie Cleghorn. The young Princess will obtain a governess in England, and on returning will visit the principal cities of the United States. . . .

On the twentieth of February, Papa Moi gave a ball at Iolani Palace to celebrate the coming-of-age of his nephew and ward, Prince David Kawananakoa. Despite the difference in their ages, Kaiulani and "Koa" had always been close. It was almost like saying farewell to her own childhood to look on while debonair David took official leave of his.

Late in April, tragic news from Molokai was brought to harbor by the little steamer *Mokolii*. At Kalaupapa, the colony where the lepers dwelt in banishment, their devoted shepherd Father Damien had died of the cruel disease. His sixteen years of selfless toil to comfort victims shut away from the outer world had earned widespread reverence, and general mourning for him saddened the kingdom. So soon to be banished herself (although for no such grim reason!), Kaiulani found a special poignancy in the plight of the exiles left without him.

Only a week later came word of another death, and this one

connected with the family. Early on a bright Tuesday morning, old Mrs. Dominis had died at Washington Place. Flags throughout the city were placed at half-staff in token of respect. With Papa, Kaiulani attended the funeral held at the imposing mansion two afternoons later. Young though she was, she could sense that in many ways this death marked the passing of an era. The grim old lady had witnessed great changes in Hawaii since first her captain brought her to a semi-savage archipelago.

Papa brought home from town news that at least the sports devotees of Honolulu would remember Kaiulani in her coming absence. In a case in the Hawaiian News Company's window, a gold baseball was on display—the trophy for the 1889 Islands Championship. And a new club—captained by that vigorous athlete Clarence Crabbe, and named in her honor "The Kaiulanis"—had been admitted to the league, to compete with four longer-established adversaries.

Then April was over. On the very last day of the month, Papa made another announcement to the newspapers: "Hon. A. S. Cleghorn, Collector General of Customs, will accompany his daughter Princess Kaiulani on her foreign journey as far as San Francisco, leaving here May 10."

Ever sensitive to her moods, Mr. Stevenson must have guessed her dread when he borrowed her red plush autograph album and wrote in it his second poem indited to Hawaiian royalty:

> Forth from her land to mine she goes,
> The island maid, the island rose,
> Light of heart and bright of face,
> The daughter of a double race.
>
> Her islands here in southern sun
> Shall mourn their Kaiulani gone,
> And I, in her dear banyan's shade,
> Look vainly for my little maid.
>
> But our Scots islands far away
> Shall glitter with unwonted day,
> And cast for once their tempest by
> To smile in Kaiulani's eye.

To this he had added a tender postscript:

> Written in April to Kaiulani in the April of her age, and at
> Waikiki within easy walk of Kaiulani's banyan. When she comes
> to my land and her father's and the rain beats upon the window
> (as I fear it will) let her look at this page; it will be like a weed
> gathered and preserved at home; and she will remember her own
> islands, and the shadow of the mighty tree; and she will hear the
> peacocks screaming in the dusk and the wind blowing in the palms.

On May 2, in her public role as a Princess of the Blood, she
dressed in her finest to accompany Papa on a first round of the
necessary formal calls of farewell. For these excursions, which
continued throughout the few days remaining before her departure, the two Cleghorns were driven in Mama's long unused
but still impressive carriage of state. It was drawn by a handsome pair of bay horses from the Fashion Stables, with a dignified driver handling the reins and a footman on the box.

In solemn succession, foreign consulates and government residences were visited. Hands were shaken. Wishes for *bon voyage*
were politely acknowledged. The King's enemies would be given
no opportunity to sneer at a lack of protocol on the part of the
youngest member of his family! On the following day, more consulates and the Cabinet members and Supreme Court Justices
were called upon, along with Oahu College, St. Andrew's Priory,
and Kawaiahao Seminary.

On Saturday, they drove out to bid several less formal good-
bys. These included one at the Stevenson villa and another at the
Heydtmann house, where Kaiulani sat on the veranda holding
her beloved Miss Gardinier's baby on her lap while the two bade
each other tearful farewells.

On Monday, the climax of the whole formal leave-taking was
reached in solemn visits to Mama and Papa Moi at the palace,
and to Aunt Liliu, still in mourning for her mother-in-law at
Washington Place. But the saddest farewell of all was a private
one. She had to ride Fairy for a last time and rub the soft muzzle
and offer a final lump of sugar and watch a groom lead away the
friend of all her childhood years.

Then Friday was upon her. The *Umatilla* was to sail for California at noon. An immense crowd had gathered at the Oceanic wharf long before the Cleghorn carriage drove in from Waikiki. The deck of the ship was crowded almost to suffocation, the traditional flower leis heaped high on the shoulders of departing residents and visitors.

When Kaiulani walked up the gangplank, the band on the dock below broke into the national anthem, "Hawaii Ponoi." As she and Annie and Papa stood at the railing alongside Mrs. Walker and her two small children, Clement and Beatrice, the whole shoreline seemed a garden of fluttering handkerchiefs and tear-wet cheeks. One of the last faces to fade into anonymity was Miss Gardinier's (impossible, still, to think of her by any other name!) whose farewell lei circled her pupil's throat.

The "all ashore" was sounded. The ship was moving. The siren of H.B.M.S. *Cormorant,* anchored in harbor, shrilled a weird accompaniment to the fading music of the band. With frightening speed, the wharf receded to toy size. Home, Hawaii, all Kaiulani's world, fell away behind her.

BOOK II

Princess in Exile

10: Over the Seas and Far Away

To Kaiulani, the world outside her Islands was a miracle of size and change.

Despite her seafaring Polynesian ancestry, she discovered during the *Umatilla*'s week-long progress toward San Francisco that she herself was not a good sailor. Much of the trip she spent wretchedly in her berth.

Notwithstanding a careful instruction in geography, and Mama's remembered descriptions, Kaiulani had not really comprehended that San Francisco could be so vastly larger than Honolulu. Days passed in a flurry of sight-seeing expeditions and entertainments by family friends. Then it was time to board the train for the east—the first real train Kaiulani had ever seen—and to say farewell to Papa, remaining behind. The tears *would* come then.

If San Francisco had been bewildering, the cities beyond the great Mississippi were—the proper word was incredible. Chicago. And then New York. Riding from the station to the Brevoort House, she gaped at the crowds, the maze of streets, the snarl of carriages on every avenue, the number and size of the fashionable shops. For none of these had she been prepared by peaceful Ainahau—or by Papa Moi's palace, which so recently she had believed to be the largest building in the world.

Even New York was no more than a brief interruption of their eastward journey. As their steamer for Liverpool passed through what Mrs. Walker called "the Narrows," Kaiulani steeled herself for misery ahead. But, to her delight, only the first few days of this second voyage were made uncomfortable for her by the ship's roll. After that she was on deck again, basking in the sun, breathing the salt air, and increasingly eager to set foot upon that other island Papa had called home.

(It was about at this time, although she could not know it, that Robert Louis Stevenson was writing of her, from his little work shack at Waikiki, to an old friend named Low whom he had known in Paris: ". . . If you want to cease to be a republican, see my little Kaiulani as she goes through. . . . I wear the colours of that little royal maiden, *Nous allons chanter à la ronde, si vous voulez!* Only she is not blonde by several chalks, though she is but a half blood, and the wrong half Edinburgh Scots like mysel'. But, O Low, I love the Polynesian. . . .")

And so she came to those "Scots islands far away" of which her banyan-tree companion had written in her book with red plush covers.

Landed at Liverpool, Kaiulani and her companions did not remain in the port city even long enough to explore it, but set out at once by train for Manchester, where they spent their first night in England. And Manchester was only an overnight stop en route to London, where they arrived on June 18. For a month and eight days she had been on the road from home to this city where history came alive.

The days were too short to accommodate the places to be seen in them. St. Paul's Cathedral; the Houses of Parliament, so vastly more impressive than the simple chambers of the Legislature back home; Westminster Abbey, where kingly dead lay in a splendor undreamed of at the damp little Royal Mausoleum in Nuuanu Valley. . . .

There was no end to the marvels of London. She was taken to ride on the city's underground railway, and blushed to recall how "modern" she had recently considered the mule trams from Honolulu to Waikiki. She was led through the art galleries, which inspired her with a great longing to paint fine pictures herself. She was chaperoned to as many of the theaters as were offering performances considered appropriate; and sat wishing that Papa Moi (who always so thoroughly enjoyed a good play) might be in the box beside her. She was taken to the famed Crystal Palace, surely one of the seven wonders of the present-day world.

Most impressive of all was the Tower of London. Every corner of the old prison-palace spoke of stories which until now had seemed fiction—the beheading of Queen Anne Boleyn, the dark murders of the two Little Princes, the imprisonment of dashing Sir Walter Raleigh.

But not all of London's celebrities were among the dead. The Shah of Persia was visiting the English capital, and occasion was made to see this glittering Dignity as he was driven past. On another afternoon, Queen Victoria herself (so long a true friend of Hawaiian royalty) went by in her carriage. She was like a tiny doll in a bonnet, bobbing along. People said her carriage springs had been especially constructed to give her an appearance of bowing to the greetings of the crowd, now she was so very old and tired. On this particular afternoon, Her Majesty was on her way to afternoon tea with the beautiful, deaf Princess of Wales at Marlborough House; and Kaiulani's thoughts flashed back to the days of the Jubilee when, as Aunt Liliu had written home, the Prince of Wales himself had escorted Mama Moi to the gala at Buckingham Palace.

On July 12, from Blackheath, she wrote to Mama Moi in dashing purple ink, trying to describe the exciting weeks. "We are going to Tenby on the 19th and expect to stay there about a week. . . ." (And, after Tenby, to visit other places for as long as the mellow summer weather continued.) "I am going to school in the middle of September, the name of the school is Great Harrowden Hall in North Hamptonshire. . . ."

Great Harrowden Hall! Never, never was she likely to forget her first glimpse of that proud old house, outside Wellingborough and sixty-odd miles from London. It stood in its park, at the end of a quarter-mile driveway, three-storied and formal and handsome. It had been built in the fifteenth century, she was told, as the seat of the Barons Vaux. During the Persecutions this distinguished Catholic family had concealed several fugitive priests in their manor. There were secret chambers romantically whispered of by the other girls. And now, centuries later, the noble heirs had leased their homeplace as a young ladies' school to its preceptress, Mrs. Sharp.

There was a double novelty, in such a setting, for a girl whose previous study had been supervised by devoted governesses, to be attending classes with other students. In the excitement of her first weeks at the school, even letters from home seemed less engrossing that the innovations which slowly became everyday routine. (One such letter from Papa carried a name which meant nothing to her at the time, although much later it was to stand in her thoughts alongside that of Satan himself. *John L. Stevens.* Papa wrote that this gentleman, a native of Maine, had arrived in Honolulu to replace Mr. Merrill as United States Minister.)

Those first Christmas holidays away from home—spent in London—inevitably brought wistful memories of Ainahau. Yet the days were, actually, far from unhappy. During them she had a very pleasant visit with Kawananakoa. Very much the young man of the world and even more handsome than she remembered, he was in England—as she was herself—for what Papa Moi considered a proper education for Hawaiian royalty.

Koa was, of course, far more blasé than she about foreign schooling. After being tutored at home by Alatau Atkinson and then attending Punahou School, he and his brothers had studied at San Mateo Military School in California—the school from which poor Edward had come home to die. Yet Koa, despite all his dashing sophistication, confessed to her privately that he too was homesick and would like to go back to Honolulu. Kuhio, who was in England with him, was away from London somewhere for the holidays; so Kaiulani did not see him.

Christmas interval was, in fact, such a success that at its close she returned unwillingly to her classes. By now, the novelty of school had worn thin. But she still had dedication to duty to see her past the bleak winter months with which a new term commenced. She could write to Mama Moi, on the first day of March, "Since I have come back to school, I have worked as hard as I could and now I am third in my French class. My lessons are rather hard but I like them better than I did when I left home. I really like to learn them. . . ."

Her reaction to the bite of this first English winter was also conscientiously reported to the Queen: "We have had some very cold weather, I rather like it when you can roast yourself by the fire but it is no joke out in the open air. I think I would like it moderately cold, not quite as cold as it is now. I wonder what we would do if we had it as cold at home as it is here. . . ." (At home, right now, surfriders would be shouting down the reef waves. The gardens at Ainahau would be glories of bloom. It seemed so far away!)

Her lessons progressed so well that by early May—shortly after Kaiulani had presented herself to the Bishop of Leicester for confirmation in the Anglican faith—Mrs. Sharp could write to Honolulu approvingly of how the small princess was applying herself.

The start of her second academic year in October 1890 found Kaiulani worrying over reports from home that Papa Moi was far from well. Friends passing through London on their way to Paris told her that the Queen was much concerned. Kaiulani painted a little picture and sent it off to her Uncle to cheer him up, and wrote separately to his wife: "I hope he will soon get well again. Please give him my love. . . ."

The recent summer holiday had ended all too quickly; for, now that it was over, she faced yet another loss. Having seen her once again installed at Great Harrowden Hall, her half-sister Annie was returning to Hawaii. On October 17, Annie departed for Southport, there to embark upon the *Servia* the following morning. And Kaiulani, left behind, had never felt so alone in all her life. But as the month wore on, a worrisome mystery arose to divert some of her thoughts from loneliness. She received a letter from the King, so obliquely phrased that much of its meaning was a riddle. Obviously, Papa Moi—in addition to questioning her about her life at school—also was warning her to be on guard against certain enemies he did not feel free to name in writing. But why? Whom did he fear?

She wrote back at once, expressing her puzzlement: "I am

quite at a loss to know to whom you refer as 'not to be relied upon'—I wish you would speak more plainly, as I cannot be upon my guard unless I know to whom you allude. . . ." She added, "Mr. Davies [ruddy-faced, dependable Mr. Theophilus Davies, whose factoring firm was one of the giant business houses of Honolulu and who thus divided his time between the Islands and his native England] took lunch with us last Wednesday. He was very kind and gave me an invitation to visit him. . . ."

The mystery tantalized her. There was nothing for it but to await her uncle's answer to her request for plainer speaking.

But the answer, which she had not for a moment doubted receiving, never came. Letters from home told instead of the public celebration of Papa Moi's birthday on November 18, with an afternoon reception at the palace; with a fine regatta, for which most of Honolulu crowded down to the wharves; with a grand display of fireworks.

Later, Kaiulani was informed that the King was leaving for a visit to the United States and had named Aunt Liliu as Regent in his absence. Auntie had done all she could to argue against this journey, since her brother was still in uncertain health. But Papa Moi was deeply concerned about the effect of the new McKinley Act, recently passed by the United States Congress, upon the sugar planters of his little kingdom. This bill (said the newspapers) awarded a subsidy per pound upon sugar domestically produced within the United States. Foreign sugar, such as Hawaii's, thus would suffer in price competition. Papa Moi remembered the splendid business results of his visit to Washington in the days of President Grant, and now was convinced that he must go there again.

A United States man-of-war, the *Charleston,* lay in Honolulu harbor at the time. Its commander, Rear Admiral George Brown —a long-time personal friend—had offered this means of transportation to San Francisco and Papa Moi had accepted willingly. Letters describing the sailing were scarcely in Kaiulani's hands before the London papers were publishing its incredible sequel.

The King of Hawaii was dead.

Upon his arrival in San Francisco, he had been taken to that hospitable city's heart and at first had seemed improved in health. But suddenly he had collapsed. He had lain for a brief time, half conscious, in his suite at the Palace Hotel. On January 20 he was dead. And by virtue of that miracle, the Transatlantic cable, word was in London by next day, long before anyone in isolated Hawaii could know it.

Theophilus Davies, who by now had supplanted Mrs. Walker as Kaiulani's guardian in England, came for her at once and took her with him to the Davies home called Sunset, at Hesketch Park, Southport. He was red with indignation at the published cause of Kalakaua's death.

"Bright's disease! It wasn't any such ailment that killed the man! The constant efforts to undermine him by some of those fine business gentlemen in Honolulu—the humiliations—the intrigues—"

Sunset was a refuge, however temporary; and from there, on the evening of January 21, 1891, Kaiulani wrote a letter home on black-bordered notepaper to Aunt Liliu, the last one left now of all Mama's people.

Dear Auntie:

I have only just heard the sad news from San Francisco. I cannot tell you my feelings just at present, but Auntie you can think how I feel. I little thought when I said goodbye to my dear Uncle nearly two years ago that it would be the last time I should see his dear face. Please give my love to Mamma Moi. . . .

The soul of kindness, Mr. Davies arranged for her own use of the cable in telegraphing San Francisco to direct that a wreath of orchids be placed upon Papa Moi's coffin there, bearing the tender message: *Aloha me ka paumake* (My love is with the one who is done with dying). There was some scrap of comfort in knowing that he who always had loved his kingly leis would not be without family flowers now, while he lay waiting (as San Francisco dispatches said he lay) for the *Charleston* to put to sea again, this time Hawaii-bound.

The snow which had fallen in late January was melted to gray

slush long before news from Honolulu could arrive. Then the letters said the *Charleston* had sailed into harbor on January 29,
bearing the King's remains. There had been no warning in the
Islands of the blow that was to fall. All the city was decked in
colorful buntings such as had welcomed Kalakaua home from
his earlier journeyings.

"It was reported," wrote Auntie, "that the ship was in sight
with yards cock-billed, in token of mourning. My ministers were
assembled in the Blue Room of the palace; and I could see
on each countenance apprehension of the fate which we
feared. . . ."

"*My* ministers . . ." In such tiny, inadvertant hints as this did
the great events which were altering Hawaii reveal themselves to
Kaiulani, far from home. Trifles spoke to her more clearly than
headlines. Auntie—Mama's elder sister, Mrs. John Owen Dominis, Princess Liliuokalani—was now Her Majesty, Queen
Liliuokalani!

March began as February ended, wet and cheerless, with the
sky above the school buildings dull as pewter by day and the
stars sponged out by night. If the winter cold lessened at all, it
was merely to give way to a new kind of chill. At home, Papa
Moi's state funeral was over. On the sixth of March she had a
letter from Koa, from his school at Cirencester, asking if she had
been recalled to Honolulu because of the family tragedy. She answered at once on the mourning stationery:

Dear Kawananakoa:
    Thank you very much for the kind letter which I received yester-
day. As I have not had any home letters by the last mail, and I have
no instructions to return home at present, I may have letters next
week—and if I do go home, I will let you know. How do you like
Cirencester, and what is Kuhio doing? . . .

When further news from Honolulu finally did arrive, it was
news formally affecting her own future. On March 9, one hour
before noon, the members of the Hawaiian House of Nobles had
gathered in the throne room at Iolani Palace. Her Majesty the
Queen had come there to meet them, on the arm of her husband
Governor Dominis—now elevated in title to Prince Consort.

Escorting them were the gentlemen of the Cabinet, her chamberlain, and four military aides. A brief opening prayer was offered by Noble Kauhane. Then Her Majesty had addressed them, reading a prepared speech.

"Nobles of My Kingdom: I have called you together to deliberate on a grave matter of State. Article Twenty-Two of the Constitution calls upon me to appoint a successor to the throne. The same Article calls for the approval of your Honorable Body of my appointment.

"I now announce to you Our beloved Niece, Her Royal Highness Victoria Kawekiu Lunalilo Kalaninuiahilapalapa Kaiulani, as my successor to the Throne of the Kingdom, and I hope that your deliberations will lead you to approve of my appointment."

The Household Guards were drawn up before one side of the entrance to the palace, and Captain Berger's band before the other, when—a few moments before noon—the Chief of Staff (Helen Cleghorn's husband, James Boyd), attended by Majors Holt and Bertlemann, rode through the streets of Honolulu to proclaim publicly the Heiress Apparent. Salutes fired from the shore batteries to solemnize the occasion were answered by the royal twenty-one guns from the United States ship-of-war *Mohican,* anchored in the harbor.

The announcement came to Kaiulani as no surprise, for Papa Moi's will had directed that she be declared heir to the throne next in line after Auntie; and that, following her, should be "His Royal Highness David Kawananakoa and the heirs of his body." Still, the actual public proclamation carried a gravity that was almost frightening.

The month was almost out before newspapers commenting on the ceremony could arrive from the Islands. There had not been anywhere a single dissenting voice. Even the *Commercial Advertiser,* so often critical of the Throne, now voiced only approval:

> The nomination of Her Royal Highness Princess Victoria Kaiulani as Heir Apparent to the throne, will receive the hearty endorsement of the entire population, native and foreign. Her mother was the Princess Royal Likelike, wife of Hon. A. S. Cleghorn, who

had already been proclaimed as second in the line of succession to the throne. The Princess Kaiulani being the only child of Likelike becomes the natural and lawful heir to her mother's right to the throne. She is now in England, or rather was at the latest date, pursuing her studies, and if she is allowed to continue them as was the plan when she left here for two or three years in England and America, it ought to give her the foundation of an enlightened and liberal education which will fit her for the high position which she is destined to fill.

11: A Visit from Papa

News from home soon made it evident that, as Queen, Auntie was to have a stormy time. The haole business powers in her realm still held its reins. Preparing to form her new Cabinet, Auntie was met by this Opposition's determination to force their own members upon her. She won a Supreme Court ruling affirming her right to name her own ministers, and courageously selected men she could trust to defend the interests of the true Hawaiian people. ("She has shown herself," read Kaiulani from the sympathetic *Bulletin*'s account of the matter, "a queen worthy of the nation. . . .")

In England, Mr. Davies—upon whom Kaiulani depended ever more heavily for explanation of events at home—predicted trouble. "We can look ahead, I fear," he said, "to even more serious clashes between your aunt and men who are reaping the best fruits of Hawaii without even becoming Hawaiian subjects. If any one figure in all the Islands can be said to be approved by everyone, that person is the new heiress apparent. You already are rendering a great service to Hawaii, merely by being your own well-beloved self."

That Northamptonshire winter yielded slowly to spring, while Kaiulani awaited further news. Able now to take long walks again, she and her schoolmates could watch a softer season invading their park at Great Harrowden Hall and marching in across all the distant fields. In May came word from home more

85

exciting than any politics. Papa wrote that he intended to come to England by midsummer for a family reunion! The thought of seeing him again filled all her days.

With June, the haying season began through all the rural shires, and scythes swung in the sunlight like the swords of a thousand make-believe battles. As the school year drew to its close, anticipation grew in her. Papa would be on his way so soon now! On his way!

Affectionate letters, both from him and from Aunt Liliu, arrived with welcome regularity, Papa's filled with plans, Auntie's containing few indications of uneasiness about the Downtown Party's machinations. In accordance with ancient custom, a new ruler of Hawaii always made a royal tour throughout the Islands of the realm, and Auntie wrote that she was undertaking this journey as a series of briefer trips. "I visited Hawaii, Maui and Molokai. At all the places on these islands where we stopped, we were most cordially greeted and royally entertained. . . ."

At last it was July, and summer heat shimmered over England. On July 27, at three in the morning, Papa actually arrived in London and registered at the Royal Hotel. He rested there a few hours and then set out directly for Great Harrowden Hall. He arrived at four in the afternoon, and as Kaiulani raced to meet him the years fell away.

Although the time in England had altered her considerably, it was difficult for her to see any change in Papa. The same commandingly tall figure she remembered held out his arms to her. The same brown eyes under beetling brows smiled for her. There he stood, her very own Papa!

At two o'clock on the following afternoon, after Papa had thoroughly inspected the school and exerted his impressive charm upon Mrs. Sharp and her assistant mistresses, he and Kaiulani started together for London. Papa had engaged rooms for them in the Langdon Hotel in Regent Street for the duration of his stay. With them went a lady companion engaged on Mrs. Sharp's specific recommendation, to chaperone Kaiulani.

With Papa in residence, the Langdon became a rallying point

for all Honolulu visitors passing through the city. Lunches and dinners became a parade of names and faces out of the past.

One afternoon, a governess brought the two Parker girls to call. It was especially exciting to be with two of her erstwhile playmates again, although at first she scarcely recognized Eva and Helen in the worldly young ladies they had become while she still was sheltered in a prim school. She wrote to Aunt Liliu, "They are both very handsome, nice girls. I think they are a little too old for me as yet, I am only a child compared with them. . . ."

As might have been expected, Papa had brought with him from home a variety of royal commissions to be executed in London. He called at the Foreign Office with letters from the Queen; but on that particular day the Prime Minister, Lord Salisbury, was visiting Queen Victoria at Windsor. The Honorable Mr. Barrington, His Lordship's private secretary, received him and was most courteous. On August 1 there arrived at the hotel a note from Mr. Barrington enclosing cards for their entire party to visit the Houses of Parliament, Windsor Castle, the Royal Gardens, and other restricted places of interest.

Another chore Auntie had delegated to her brother-in-law was the selection of a diamond star. Having made canny Scots inquiries as to which among the reliable jewelers gave best value, Papa settled upon the Goldsmith Alliance Limited and visited their offices. By August 5, they had sent him sketches of three possible designs for the jewel. Papa relayed them to Honolulu, along with a businesslike hint that terms were net cash and that if "dear Lydia" would send him the money he would do for her the very best he could.

Papa's long, wistful wish to see his native Scotland again was fulfilled, with Kaiulani as an eager companion. A long-time friend of her family, the Honorable R. A. McFee, invited them for a ten-day visit to his Dreghorn Castle at Collington. While they were under his roof, their host honored them by flying the flag of Hawaii from his castle tower. The Scottish breezes must have found it an old familiar, for, on his trip around the world,

Papa Moi also had been entertained at Dreghorn Castle. While he was there, Kalakaua had planted two trees. And at Mr. Mc-Fee's request, Kaiulani followed her uncle's example and planted another.

Together, too, she and her father visited the glowing Highlands dear to Archibald Cleghorn's memory, and the cities of Glasgow and Edinburgh. History crowded in on them here especially close. Kaiulani was shown the shirt and watch and a lock of the hair of King Charles I, executed (uneasy thought!) by rebellious subjects. She inspected with interest the original Act of Union of Scotland and England, and was allowed to handle a book actually written in by "Good Queen Bess."

Returning to London by way of Wales, they were guests en route of Lord and Lady Brassey at their ancestral seat, Normanhurst. Here they were taken to the home of that great among the greatest of prima donnas, Mme. Adelina Patti. Back in England, Kaiulani and Papa devoted almost an entire week to the gala naval maneuvers at Portsmouth, in which the vessels of the French fleet took part. And then—London once more.

The perfection of these passing weeks was flawed only by the unfortunate state of Papa's health. He had caught a severe cold on the voyage from New York, and after some initial improvement suffered a relapse because of this climate he had not known since boyhood. Even a visit with the hospitable Davies family at Sundown, overlooking the Irish Sea, did not rid Papa altogether of his miseries.

Auntie, it seemed, had been anxious about the condition of her niece's never-strong eyesight. So, while Papa was consulting doctors about his own ailment, appointments with eye specialists were added to the Cleghorns' schedule. Papa then wrote to his wife's sister, "Kaiulani . . . can read all right but she cannot see without glasses any object a few feet away. She is nearsighted, and I am afraid will remain so. I will give you full particulars on my return. . . ."

The weeks of his visit seemed to melt like snows in spring. September came, and the mails from home brought sad news indeed.

On August 27 Auntie's beloved John Dominis, failing to rally from an illness, had died while she sat at his bedside in Washington Place. "Just at the time I was to need most greatly his guiding hand . . ." the heartbroken widow wrote. So soon after Papa Moi's funeral, reports from the Islands were again of a lying-in-state at the palace. With her gentle husband gone, Aunt Liliu was truly alone. Writing immediately, Kaiulani was still too dazed to say what was in her heart. But later, from Sundown, she tried again: "I know that my last letter was very short and abrupt, but my dear Auntie, I really could not find words to express my grief. . . ."

Rumors already were adrift in England, among their own friends with Island connections, that almost certainly the Queen would appoint Kawananakoa to the governorship of Oahu left vacant by the Prince Consort's death. Considerably distressed, Kaiulani wrote yet again in Papa's behalf: "I hear from many people that David is to have the governorship, please do not think me very forward, but I should so like Father to have it. I have not asked you for anything before, but if you can possibly grant this, I should be so very grateful. . . ."

The days of Papa's visit already were almost over. Now only a week remained before October 3, when he would sail for New York aboard the Cunard steamer *Umbria*. On Monday of that week, the victim of his ever-lively curiosity, Papa went into the slums of London with a police detective to observe how the law-enforcers of the greatest metropolis in the world went about their work. He did not return home until after one in the morning, and then in such condition a doctor had to be summoned. It was the medical opinion that the sordid smells of the area explored had been too much for a visitor.

But despite misadventures, their good times continued right up until the last. One evening they went to dine with the distinguished young dramatist, Mr. John Millington Synge, who seemed to Kaiulani a most agreeable gentleman and who had much warm praise to bestow upon poor Uncle John. Their old Hawaii friends, Sir William and Lady Wiseman, and the Parker girls, came to dinner with them on the last Wednesday.

And then Papa's visit was over. The boat sailed and Kaiulani was back in the familiar, ordered life of Great Harrowden Hall. Holding back her tears, she again wrote to Auntie. About Papa: "You can fancy how lonely I shall feel without him. . . . I have been so very happy these last few weeks I do not know how I shall be able to settle down to my lessons again . . ." About the future in general, and hope for a summons home: "I am going to study as hard as I possibly can. . . . When I come home I shall try to help you as much as I possibly can, tho' it will not be much as I do not understand state affairs. . . ."

Hints. Broad hints. Yet with a new school year well under way, there was still no queenly command for her return to Hawaii. With 1892 already dying, it diverted her from her impatient waiting to share with her British schoolmates the early December excitement of a royal engagement.

"Prince Eddy"—Duke of Clarence and Avondale, and heir after his father the Prince of Wales to Queen Victoria's crown— was to marry the Princess Mary of Teck, his distant cousin. The proposal had taken place during a gay house party at Luton Hoo, the Bedfordshire house of Danish Minister de Falbe; and through all the British Isles each new development was eagerly followed.

Poor little Hawaii! How long had it been since such whole-hearted general devotion had been shown—at least by many in the realm—to her reigning family? Yet Kaiulani could have asked no better Christmas gift than permission to return at once to her troubled Island home.

12: An Empty Throne

The holidays that year brought exciting family news. At Waikiki, Papa was building a new Ainahau, replacing the old house with a more handsome one. Writing from Southport to Aunt Liliu, Kaiulani exulted: "I'm so glad. . . . It has always been my ambition to have a house at Waikiki worthy of the beautiful gardens."

The new year, arriving, brought with it foul weather and murky yellow fog. As if empathically, England's royal engagement took a somber and finally a tragic turn. On January 14, the young Duke died of pneumonia following a sudden lung congestion. The country was desolated. Shops everywhere put up their shutters. Churchbells tolled. The girls at Great Harrowden Hall learned a sad ballad, apparently composed overnight to the tune of "God Bless the Prince of Wales," and along with the others, Kaiulani found herself lamenting:

> A nation wrapped in mourning
> Shed bitter tears today
> For the noble Duke of Clarence
> And fair young Princess May. . . .

Instead of a wedding, a funeral was held at Windsor on January 20. Princess Mary's bridal wreath was laid upon her lost Duke's coffin, and the young ladies of Great Harrowden Hall wept their eyes red.

Abruptly, now, Kaiulani's days were completely altered. Mr.

Davies had decided (and had persuaded her family to agree) that she should leave Northamptonshire for good. She was to continue her studies with private instructors at Brighton, Sussex, where a chaperone was found.

Mrs. Rooke—that name so familiar to Hawaiian royalty, since it had been half-English Queen Emma's own before her marriage to King Kamehameha IV—was a delightful gentlewoman, who from the first acted as a proxy mother to her new charge. Auntie was soon informed that "I shall take lessons in French, German, Music and English, especially grammar and composition." But for how long must they last? "I am anxiously awaiting for the time to come when I may see you again. . . ."

By March 1 she was comfortably settled in at Mrs. Rooke's house on Cambridge Road, and finding that Brighton was a delightful place and so easy to explore that it quickly became familiar. The salt air off the English Channel was pure and bracing and did instant wonders for her appetite. She was soon fairly glowing with energy.

The curriculum she had described for the Queen almost from the first was augmented to include singing. Her singing mistress she found particularly pleasant and encouraging, and Auntie soon was told that "She has taught me such a lot, and she says that I have a very sweet soprano voice. I think that I must have inherited it from you. . . ."

During this early spring, Kaiulani discovered the joys of amateur stamp collecting and spent many evenings filling her new album. From Hawaii, Mr. Charles Bishop sent her a new book by Prof. W. D. Alexander, *A Brief History of the Hawaiian People*. She read this book with a keen interest and a growing surprise at how little she had known about the past of her own Islands.

Alice Davies, her guardian's daughter, had come down to Brighton to be with her. Many vacation visits to the Davies home had made Alice seem like a sister, and they were nearly enough of an age (although Alice was somewhat older) to be completely congenial. The days flowed past.

Letters and newspapers told her of Auntie's continuing struggles with her haole enemies. Kaiulani read with relief that the Royalists had won a slim majority in both houses in the campaigns for the 1892 Legislature, but loyalty seemed to have a malignant foe in Hawaii's current United States minister. Denying all proper diplomatic behavior, John L. Stevens had declared himself publically as standing ready to give all aid he could to the factions clamoring to annex Hawaii to the United States. Friends who knew the man, passing through England, told her the Maine Yankee had in the past been variously a Christian minister, a newspaper man, and a rabble-rousing politician. He was known to be a fanatical advocate of American imperialism.

In Sussex, popular appreciation of royalty seemed greater than at home. Kaiulani was beseeched by her new friends at Brighton for the Queen's autograph. But she was unwilling to snip it from any of Auntie's treasured letters, and such requests were always refused.

After so long a wait, plans for her return home were actually in the making. As she understood it, she was to remain in England until perhaps the Christmas season, then travel on the Continent for a month or two, before making her debut in society. This would, of course, include her formal presentation to Queen Victoria. After that (certainly within the year!) there would come the anticipated summons. Tremulously, she wrote, "I am looking forward to my return. . . . I am beginning to feel very homesick."

Christmas was still months away, however. Spring holiday was near at hand. This year, it was to be spent on Jersey—one of those tiny islands, almost across the Channel, which the French writer Victor Hugo had called "pieces broken off France." She and Mrs. Rooke sailed from Southampton at midnight on April 20. Poor sailor that she was, Kaiulani dreaded the nine-hour passage. And the Channel's reputation for roughness proved justified. They were a full two hours behind schedule when they docked at St. Helier next day, and Kaiulani had been violently ill almost from the start of the voyage. But the drive from St. Helier to Rozel, where Mrs. Rooke's house La Chaire stood, was all that was needed to refresh her.

Quaint St. Helier, the island's only town of any size, beguiled her from the first. Mrs. Rooke explained that the pious St. Helerius had lived on an unsheltered rock offshore, devoting an isolated life to prayer, until marauding Norsemen had butchered him. The village on a marsh close by had adopted his martyred name as its own.

Rozel was six miles from St. Helier but only two from St. Martyn's, where their post office was located and where they went to church. On the first Sunday, Kaiulani walked twice to services. Morning devotions were in French, the language of the island, and she discovered with pride that she could understand quite well all that was said. The church itself was very old and would have been lovely, she thought, if someone had not "modernized" it by facing the old stone tower with cement.

Jersey weather, she quickly discovered, was close to perfection. And the island's coastline, like those of Hawaii's islands, was indented with frequent little bays and bold rocky headlands. A girdle of rocks surrounded everything, much like the reefs at home, jutting above the bluest of waters. And seaward from Rozel Bay, with its tiny pier and its fleet of fishing boats, the distant coast of France could be seen beyond black rocks like sleeping whales. Kaiulani wrote to Auntie: ". . . and altogether this place reminds me very much of home. I wish I was there now."

In almost every one of Jersey's tiny bays, the ruin of a tower or fort stood guard—relics of invasions since the dawn of time. Celts, Romans, Normans—all had assailed these shores. At low tide, in such bays as St. Ouen's or St. Clement's, one could see the vast treetrunks of a forest drowned millenniums ago. The bones of the mammoth, the wooly rhinoceros, and the prehistoric reindeer all had been uncovered here—relics centuries older than the very oldest *heiau* or burial cave of Hawaii. ("Auntie, I do want to stay here for two or three months instead of only two weeks! Perhaps we may come over again. . . .")

The two weeks were gone almost like the catch of a breath.

The passage back to England was, perversely, as smooth as a canoe ride on a sheltered pond. They were back again at Seven Cambridge Road, and it was mid-May. Mr. Davies came, bringing Alice with him for another visit. Approaching summer warmed Sussex, and the girls could wear thin blouses.

Auntie was assured that "the only thing that I miss is my riding horse. I would give almost everything if I could have Fairy to ride. . . . I am having such very pretty summer dresses made. I do like pretty, dainty things. All the ladies are wearing dresses made like men's clothes. I do dislike them so, they look so very manly. . . ."

By now, in Honolulu, the new Legislature was well into its session. Political reports from home all were of verbal violence and struggle. Public quarrels between Royalists and Reformers in the sessions grew wildly heated. Auntie's loyal attorney general, Mr. Paul Neumann, remarked that they were "better than a circus—and it's free!" But the constant strain could scarcely have been a circus for poor Auntie.

The Queen's opening address to the Legislature had called for many government economies, including a voluntary cut of ten thousand dollars in her own privy purse. But enemies fought her every move. Kaiulani's own name entered the lists of battle when the appropriation necessary to continue her education was bitterly opposed—the very education originally undertaken at Mr. Thurston's urging! The Reformers, determined to restore their former stranglehold on the government, were voting cabinet after cabinet out of office "for want of confidence."

The English summer into which these disturbing tidings continued to trickle was, by contrast, deceptively serene. Kaiulani spent her holiday with the Davieses, and threw herself into the business of helping to raise funds for charity—reporting home that "I now have over four hundred pounds and hope soon to have more. I wish I could do more for good works." Ever dependable, Auntie forwarded through Papa a generous donation, encouraging in her heir the selfless activity to which she had devoted so much of her own purposeful life.

On September 17, a Saturday, Kaiulani returned to Brighton

to resume her studies. The resort town was coming alive again, its season already well begun, and on fine afternoons the Front was crowded with the carriages of "persons of note." But very few people knew that the Princess of Hawaii was one of them. In shops where she ordered parcels delivered to Mrs. Rooke's address, Kaiulani was amused to find that the salespeople took her to be a Miss Rooke and so addressed her.

Three days each week, Mr. Loman arrived to instruct Kaiulani in physics, literature, and history. Each morning, with an almost obsessive punctuality, Fräulein Kling appeared for an hour's conversation in French or German, augmented by sessions of translation. During the week Kaiulani also had two singing lessons with Madame Lancia; two painting lessons; two music lessons; and instruction in dancing, riding, and deportment. Two hours each day were required for music practice, and two more for preparing various assignments. Kaiulani had grown increasingly serious about these obligations of her education, realizing that within the year she might be home again and putting her preparation to practical use.

Auntie wrote in confidence that she had begun to consider granting a new constitution to her people. The requests for such a move were increasing almost daily. A bill had been introduced in the Legislature, calling for a constitutional convention to do away with that unjust property-owning restriction which robbed most native Hawaiians of the vote. Petitions were begging the Queen to follow the example of Lot Kamehameha in 1864 in establishing a new constitution by royal fiat. These appeals were signed by thousands of the fairer-minded haoles, as well as by the native Hawaiians.

Kaiulani dreaded to think what those powerful foreign businessmen might do, once aroused to the Queen's intentions. But such worries, although real enough, cast no particular shadow over her autumn as it brightened and then faded.

Auntie was not so preoccupied with affairs of state as to forget her niece's seventeenth birthday. She sent funds for the purchase of a necklace. Writing her thanks, Kaiulani promised to shop for the suggested gift, "but not now as I do not know anyone who is a connoisseur in the matter. I shall visit the Wisemans at Christmas, then I can ask Sir William."

Early that October, she took the first of the formal lessons in dancing and general deportment, "which," she wrote home, "I found highly amusing. My friends tell me that I carry myself so much better when walking in the street than in a Drawingroom, so at the present moment I am doing my very best to walk into a room quietly and gracefully."

October wore itself out in two weeks of cold, damp drizzle which would have depressed her more save for the joy she was finding in local music. Number Seven Cambridge Road stood very near the best church in Brighton, and on evenings mild enough for leaving the windows open she could listen for hours to the choirboys practicing—an unseen chorus of a purity which did seem almost heavenly. On one particular night, when they were doing that exquisite anthem "Hymn to the Creator," she could have listened for hours after the last strains faded.

For her birthday—as Kaiulani wrote home with pleasure— Mrs. Rooke had given her a picture called "The Soul's Awakening," which she long had admired. She hung it carefully on the wall facing her bed, so that the first thing she might see in the morning was the lovely face of the girl it depicted, with the early radiance on it. Birthday letters and other gifts had arrived in abundance.

The October issue of *Paradise of the Pacific*, forwarded from Ainahau, carried an article about Kaiulani. It was headed "Hawaii's Hope," and told the story of her life with reassuring affection. "In her childhood and early school days the little princess displayed such sweetness of disposition and lovable manners that soon 'None knew her but to love her, None named her but to praise.' . . ." The article concluded on a note of confidence concerning the "return home of Hawaii's Hope, to celebrate her eighteenth birthday in the land of her race."

These days, somewhat to her dismay, Kaiulani seemed always to be writing the Queen to request some favor. Once, it was the simple matter of a royal photograph—"I have not got one of you. My room is very pretty but I think a few photos would improve it—as present I have only two, one of Mother and one of Father." But other matters were more serious, as: "I hear that you wish Father to be Governor but to give up the Custom House. Auntie, we cannot do without his salary for that, as the salary of Governor is only half the other. . . ."

She had been invited by Lady Wiseman to spend her Christmas holiday at the Priory Rittle, in Chelmsford, and happily accepted. Since his Honolulu visit as commander of H.B.M.S. *Caroline,* just after Mama's death, Sir William had been a great family favorite. Moreover, the Wisemans epitomized the very influences she had been sent to England to profit from. To Auntie she wrote, "they are gentle people and I think that it is my duty to visit people whose manners are refined, as it is quite essential for me to be well mannered."

News from home throughout the holidays continued to build her hopes higher. One of the Legislature's last acts before its session ended was the voting of four thousand dollars to cover expenses of the Heiress Apparent's return to her islands. Arrangements had been begun for her formal presentation to Queen Victoria. How could Christmas be other than perfect, with such a future immediately beyond it?

But that visit to Chelmsford seemed to mark the end of happiness. For with late January came news from Honolulu so stunning that she was never quite to recover from it. The haoles really had bared their fangs at last!

On Monday, January 30, 1893, Mr. Davies received a series of three terse telegrams. He promptly relayed their contents to her. The first of them said only, "Queen deposed." The second, equally brief, reported, "Monarchy abrogated." The third, almost like a postscript, directed, "Break news to Princess." And presently from someone in Washington, unsigned, came anonymous corroboration: "Islands transferred. Princess provided for."

That new Constitution demanded by the natives had provided that, as in other lands, only citizens of Hawaii might vote in Hawaiian elections. The foreign haoles had cried out in rage, and then had struck.

A so-called Committee of Safety, organized to overthrow the

legal government of Hawaii, had drafted a provisional government of their own which would immediately petition the United States for annexation. Volunteer rifle companies of their followers had enforced their grab for power. And a more-than-willing companion in their treachery had been that case-hardened troublemaker, United States Minister John Stevens. He had backed up the plan by boarding the American ship-of-war *Boston* (then in Honolulu harbor to discourage armed lawlessness) and sailing her off to Hilo, on the Big Island, on a flimsy pretext.

With the *Boston*'s guns no longer present to deter them, the rebels had acted swiftly. On the night of January 16 they had staged a mass meeting of their relatively few supporters, declaring this to be a "popular demand" for the overthrow of the Monarchy. Urged by her loyal marshal, C. B. Wilson, to permit him to deal with the insurgents firmly, the Queen had hesitated to sanction gunfire in Honolulu's streets.

Her indecision had cost her dearly. Once the mass meeting was over, the *Boston* had returned as inexplicably as it had departed. A gloating Minister Stevens had landed troops off her without delay, claiming that American lives and property were in danger. But the Marines had then been lined up with their guns trained upon Iolani Palace. On January 17 the provisional government had proclaimed itself, with Mr. Sanford B. Dole as its president, announcing that it would administer the government "until terms of union with the United States of America have been negotiated."

Facing those American guns so outrageously misused by Minister Stevens, Auntie had accepted the advice of her frightened Cabinet. She had surrendered her authority under protest—appealing to the United States to restore the friendly legal government thus toppled.

Two days later, five provisional-government "commissioners" were already on their way to Washington to negotiate annexation. At the time of their departure, residents of the outer islands had not yet even heard of the revolution.

To Dr. John Mott-Smith, Auntie's minister in Washington, Mr. Davies wrote at once, "Either the Washington government will accept the offer to annex or they will decline. . . . But if they accept they must also realize that no amount of reasoning, and probably no amount of bribe, will ever gain the pure Hawaiian vote; and without that vote how can Annexation be carried on? Hawaiians cannot be ignored."

A few days later, after sober thought, Kaiulani's guardian decided to advise her that the only thing she could do for her people in this grave hour was to accompany him to Washington. At first, the prospect of this battle to be fought in the full spotlight of the press terrified her. But she was a daughter of a race of warriors, and she had been well schooled to heed her duty.

She replied, "Perhaps some day the Hawaiians will say, Kaiulani, you could have saved us and you did not try. I will go with you."

13: The Uninvited

Letters from Papa, during the early weeks of February, told more than the sparse cablegrams. Together with the few other friends the Queen could trust, he had been summoned on the afternoon the provisional government was proclaimed, to advise her in her troubles. Those present had agreed that while American guns dominated Honolulu armed resistance was futile. Her Majesty had signed a formal protest, yielding her authority "until such time as the Government of the United States shall, upon the facts being presented to it, undo the action of its representative and reinstate me. . . ."

Auntie had then removed herself to Washington Place. From there she wrote to President Harrison and to President-Elect Grover Cleveland who, on the fourth of March, would again be moving into the White House. The Queen hoped much of his long friendship for her kingdom.

Meanwhile, Minister Stevens had run up an American flag over the government buildings. A totally unauthorized American protectorate was proclaimed over the provisional government, thus checking intervention by other foreign powers represented in Honolulu—all of whom, in varying degree, protested the overthrow of the lawful government.

Papa wrote that immediately following the overthrow he had called upon Lorrin Thurston—the real power of the new regime. Papa had told Mr. Thurston that, while his sister-in-law's dethronement might have some basis of justification in view of her intention to proclaim a new constitution, still the monarchy need not be overturned. With the Queen dethroned, Kaiulani (already her heir apparent) might be named queen under a board of regents appointed to act during her minority.

To this, Mr. Thurston had replied, "You know my regard for Princess Kaiulani, Mr. Cleghorn. I think very highly of her. . . . But matters have proceeded too far for your plan to be an adequate answer to this situation. We are going to abrogate the monarchy entirely."

Papa had bowed his head, tears in his eyes, and walked away. He had hoped against hope, for it was known that many in the new government (Mr. Dole among them) still favored such a regency.

By now, Mr. Paul Neumann was on his way to Washington as the Queen's envoy extraordinary. Kawananakoa was accompanying him on his mission, which was to negotiate for a withdrawal of the Annexation Treaty and to plead for a restoration of Hawaii's throne.

The representatives of the provisional government (already popularly or unpopularly known, Kaiulani heard, as "the P.G.s") had presented a hasty draft of their treaty to President Harrison on February 3. On Valentine's Day, Mr. Harrison had signed it and rushed it to the Senate for approval. Regarding the royal family the treaty's provisions were simple. The Queen was to receive an annual pension of twenty thousand dollars and Princess Kaiulani a flat grant of one hundred and fifty thousand, in satisfaction of claims to the throne. Both grants were "on condition of an unhesitating and continuous acquiescence in the abrogation of the Monarchy and the annexation of the Islands to the United States. . . ."

On February 18, harkening to Mr. Davies' counsel, Kaiulani issued a statement through the London newspapers—formally addressing it not to sympathetic English readers but to the American people:

> Four years ago, at the request of Mr. Thurston, then a Hawaiian Cabinet Minister, I was sent away to England to be educated

privately and fitted to the position which by the Constitution of Hawaii I was to inherit. For all these years I have patiently and in exile striven to fit myself for my return this year to my native country.

I am now told that Mr. Thurston is in Washington asking you to take away my flag and my throne. No one tells me even this officially. Have I done anything wrong, that this wrong should be done to me and my people? I am coming to Washington to plead for my throne, my nation and my flag. Will not the great American people hear me?

Mr. Davies booked passage on the *Teutonic* and they sailed a few days later—Kaiulani, Mr. and Mrs. Davies, their daughter Alice, a chaperone-companion named Miss Whartoff, and a maid. They arrived in New York harbor on the first day of March. After pausing briefly at the health officer's boarding station, the liner barely had gotten under way again when a revenue cutter with the name *Chandler* lettered on her bow came darting down the bay to draw alongside. Up a swaying Jacob's ladder climbed two well-remembered figures, the Queen's former Minister of Finance, Mr. E. C. Macfarlane, and her minister to Washington, Dr. John Mott-Smith. Since Dr. Mott-Smith had answered Mr. Davies' cabled offer of help with a terse "Cannot use assistance yet," his pleasure at their coming might be merely formal. Still, he had not neglected the courtesy.

The pier where the *Teutonic* presently berthed was swarming with newspaper reporters and an army of curiosity-seekers anxious for a glimpse of the Crown Princess who might someday become an American citizen, if her homeland was annexed. Said one news account, next day, "The Princess . . . is a tall, beautiful young woman of sweet face and slender figure. She has the soft, dark eyes and dark complexion that mark the Hawaiian beauty . . ." And another: "The Princess impresses one as . . . tall and slight [with] decidedly good eyes, which are a soft brown. Her hair is almost black and somewhat wavy. Her complexion is dark but not more so than many girls whom one meets every day on Broadway. She wore yesterday, when she left the steamship, a simple gray travelling gown with a dark jacket and some sort of fluffy hat which was not unbecoming. She talks in a very simple, dignified way and seems possessed of decidedly more common sense than most young women of seventeen or eighteen."

Mr. Davies had helped during the voyage to prepare a formal statement which Kaiulani read aloud to the reporters on the pier:

"Unbidden I stand upon your shores today, where I had thought so soon to receive a royal welcome. I come unattended except for the loving hearts that have come with me over the winter seas. I hear that Commissioners from my land have been for many days asking this great nation to take away my little vineyard. They speak no word to me, and leave me to find out as I can from the rumors of the air that they would leave me without a home or a name or a nation.

"Seventy years ago Christian America sent over Christian men and women to give religion and civilization to Hawaii. Today, three of the sons of those missionaries are at your capitol asking you to undo their fathers' work. Who sent them? Who gave them the authority to break the Constitution which they swore they would uphold?

"Today, I, a poor, weak girl with not one of my people near me and all these Hawaiian statesmen against me, have strength to stand up for the rights of my people. Even now I can hear their wail in my heart and it gives me strength and courage and I am strong—strong in the faith of God, strong in the knowledge that I am right, strong in the strength of seventy million people who in this free land will hear my cry and will refuse to let their flag cover dishonor to mine!"

All political questions, Mr. Davies insisted, must be addressed to him. Ruddy face earnest, he answered the reporters forcefully. As rapidly as possible, then, he hustled his party through the crowd to waiting carriages which took them eastward through the city to the remembered Brevoort House. Here, at least the ladies could retire to their chambers and rest. Mr. Davies, Mr. Macfarlane, and Dr. Mott-Smith were kept busy in the suite's parlor fending off a new battery of reporters.

Kaiulani was not summoned until evening to receive any of the constant stream of callers, and then only because a very special one awaited her in the public rooms downstairs. He had arrived with Mr. Macfarlane at half-past eight and Mr. Davies had gone down to speak with him. But (because Koa had expressed himself in Washington as opposed to her visit) it was nearly ten o'clock before Mrs. Davies allowed him to offer his respects—and then only for a visit of a few minutes.

In his light trousers and dark cutaway, her princely "cousin" seemed even handsomer than she had remembered. But despite his flawless politeness, she could detect an aloof disapproval. Although he said nothing of it in words, it was evident that he resented her having come to America. Kaiulani could guess why. He was in Washington to work with Mr. Neumann in Auntie's personal behalf. She knew that many Hawaiian royalists, even her own father and Mr. Davies, were suggesting that the only way to save the monarchy might be to persuade Queen Liliuokalani to step down and allow her niece to mount the throne under a haole regency. Kaiulani never would have consented to this, but Koa could scarcely be blamed for resenting her arrival.

During their first morning in America, callers came and went at the Davies' suite. The Thursday papers reported her arrival, but she scanned them more anxiously for other news of the Hawaiian situation. President Harrison's impending departure from Washington and President Cleveland's arrival there dominated the news columns.

During the afternoon, the new arrivals drove out in a carriage to inspect the city. The high point of the tour was a pause at the huge Seventh Regiment Armory, which Kaiulani found particularly interesting—perhaps because she had not until now seen American troops such as had stood drawn up before Iolani Palace a few weeks earlier.

The Friday morning news included a story from Washington reporting Koa's remarks after returning from his courtesy visit to New York. It hurt her to read what he had said of her. He told reporters flatly that Princess Kaiulani was working in the wrong direction and under the thumb of Theo Davies. And: "Mr. Davies is working against the interests of the Queen, which is bad taste to say the least. . . ."

It troubled her that Koa had so misunderstood the purpose of their journey. The last thing in her thoughts had been any disloyalty to Auntie. And certainly Mr. Davies was devoting all his efforts to the service of the Hawaiian monarchy. Perhaps it was one more symptom of a sick time that even those dedicated to opposing the encroachments of foreigners in Hawaii should thus be at odds.

With the approaching week end, Mr. Cleveland would become President. Washington seethed with preparations for his Inauguration, and would have little time now to consider Hawaii's fate. So Mr. Davies had arranged to take them all to visit Boston, while they waited for a new (and hopefully, a more friendly) administration to take over. They left New York by train at ten o'clock on Friday morning.

The new government at Honolulu had apparently seen to it that Boston would be warned against their arrival. Reading copies of the past week's *Globe* while their train flashed through a white New England landscape, Mr. Davies snorted over a story on a lecture entitled "Hawaii, Past and Present," given at the Young Men's Christian Union by Mr. Gorham T. Gilman. From all that Kaiulani had heard of him, this Mr. Gilman was a man who seldom dropped his bread buttered side down. For years he had fawned upon the Hawaiian monarchy. But with the change in government, he suddenly was the devoted champion of the P.G.s. His eagerness to echo their propaganda slanders of Hawaii's recent rulers was equaled, it seemed, only by his ardor in urging Hawaiian annexation to the United States.

At Providence a woman reporter from the *Globe* boarded the train and was received by Mr. and Mrs. Davies. Kaiulani was presented to her, but took little part in the interview which followed. She sat instead—in her fitted "tailor-made" of English blue serge and her large *à la mode* hat of felt trimmed with ostrich plumes—a bit removed from the talk, in one corner of the car, chatting with Alice Davies. ("As if," wrote their vistor for the next day's paper, "falling dynasties were as remote from her life as from that of any Beacon Street belle.")

Outside the train windows, Rhode Island gave way to Massachusetts. Villages and farms huddled under the snow's white weight like herds of animals caught by surprise and frozen where they stood. ("She sings very well," Mr. Davies was saying with a smile, "unless she thinks someone is listening. And then she is nervous. . . . Her mother, sister of King Kalakaua, who was in this country some fifteen years ago, was a very high-spirited woman. But Kaiulani has learned to control herself.")

March twilight was crowding in when they reached the Boston station at half-past four. The Davies' son Clive, a third-year student at the Institute of Technology, was there to meet them and they drove directly to the Hotel Brunswick, where apartments had been engaged.

The Venetian Suite had been set aside for Kaiulani's own use and that of Miss Whartoff, her temporary lady-in-waiting. Ornately paneled, it was said to be one of the handsomest accommodations in the city. Its windows looked out over Boylston Street, framing a busy panorama of activity. The Davies family occupied five rooms on the floor directly above.

For the most part, Saturday was a quiet day. No callers were received. Resting in her rooms during the morning and recovering from a slight cold brought on by the sharp weather, Kaiulani imagined the ceremonies going on in far-away Washington, where Mr. Cleveland—attended by his new Vice-President, Mr. Adlai E. Stevenson—would be taking his oath as President for a second time.

At midafternoon she ventured from the hotel for an exciting outing. Could one ever forget one's first real New England sleigh-ride—or Boston in the snow? The big, comfortable Russian sleigh ordered for the party was pulled by a sleek pair of dock-tailed bays. Kaiulani and her friends, bundled in fur robes, were driven swiftly along Beacon Street and then through Brookline and Cambridge, sleighbells jangling merrily on the crisp air. The runners beneath them slid over hard, smooth whiteness as exhilaratingly as, back home, a racing surfboard rode the reef waves.

Kaiulani and Mr. and Mrs. Davies went by sleigh again, on Sunday morning, to communion at St. Paul's church. Because her attendance had not been announced, few recognized the visiting Princess of Hawaii. But the public were aware that she intended to be present at four o'clock vespers at Trinity. This church was packed to capacity long before Mr. and Mrs. Davies escorted her across Clarendon Street to the church door ("walking," the next day's *Globe* noted approvingly, "in the most simple and democratic fashion.") They were ushered to a pew on the center aisle, some dozen rows from the front. Curious stares followed them every step of the way. Describing her arrival, the *Globe*'s reporter awarded Kaiulani the supreme accolade by writing that she had looked "quite Bostonian"!

Monday accelerated the tempo of her brief stay in the city which had sent out the first Christian missionaries to her homeland.

With Mr. Davies, she paid a morning call upon former Governor Ames and his wife, old friends of her guardian. Then they went to the studio of Elmer Chickering, considered Boston's finest photographer, to have her portrait taken; and finished the morning with a visit to Clive Davies' classrooms at the Institute of Technology, and a guided tour of its buildings.

A reception was given at the hotel during the afternoon and evening, in Kaiulani's own suite—to be described for the public as "a very fitting throne room indeed. But a very informal one, like an English drawingroom, where as dusk deepens everyone has tea." The reception was open only to those who came properly introduced—including many former Honolulu residents now living in Boston. Clive's young college friends attended in force and surrounded her like a guard of honor. One of these young men, anxious to please, told her he too had been born in the Islands.

"Why then," the smiling Kaiulani said promptly (with "a pretty little showing of sovereignty," as one reporter stood near enough to note)—"Why then, you belong to me!"

Seated among her beaux like a queen indeed, she wore a gown

patterned after the *haute couture* of 1830 now newly returning to fashion. Its ivory silk was strewn with blossoms and trailing vines in turquoise blue and its skirt trimmed with rows of turquoise satin ribbon ruching. Her dark hair was coiled at the back of her head in her favorite semi-Greek knot, and apparently the total picture was so pleasing to the "Tech" boys that they never left her side.

Representatives of every newspaper in Boston had been invited. One writer, instantly captivated, described their talk in print next morning: "The Princess begins each sentence with a demure, wholly English air, as if not feeling quite sure that it is decorous for her to express her opinion, and then loses her shyness and speaks enthusiastically till the next question, when her eyes drop and she is the shy school girl again—a manner as fetching as it is un-American."

Such personal conquest of individual reporters, however, had not thwarted the determined campaign by her Aunt's enemies to disparage the fallen monarchy. The *Globe*'s lead Tuesday editorial was a protest against the pension being proposed for Queen Liliuokalani as recompense for the usurpation of her throne and her Crown Lands revenues.

Pointing out that the widows of such American heroes as General McClellan and former President Grant were receiving smaller ones, the *Globe* scorned "the Hawaiian ex-Queen to whom we really owe nothing." Its final judgment left one stunned: "Somehow or other, this sort of procedure doesn't compare over and above favorably with the straightforward ways of other days when the strong annexed the weak by right of might and disdained to bribe anyone into pocketing the injury in silence." Was this generous, honorable America speaking? Or haole Honolulu?

On their final day in Boston they went to a suburb of the city and visited Wellesley College—the school where, in former times, it had been suggested that she might finish her education. A year at Wellesley (so family opinion had run) might silence grumbles that an English schooling could breed a ruler unsympathetic to American interests in her kingdom.

Now all such debate was dead. Yet it would have been impossible to view this handsome campus and the throngs of carefree girls inhabiting it, without some pang for what might have been. A delegation from the school met their train at the Wellesley station, and in the Browning Room at the college an official committee waited to show the Princess and Mr. and Mrs. Davies through the classrooms, art museum, science laboratory, and library.

When a gong sounded for lunch, the chief corridor of College Hall instantly filled with students released from classes. As Kaiulani walked down the stairs, on her way to the faculty parlor, they greeted her with the college cheer.

After lunch, the tour of the college was continued with another faculty escort; and when it was ended, they found the students massed again in the main hall. While a carriage waited to take the visitors to their train, the college musical club burst into a sweet-voiced singing of the Wellesley *Alma Mater,* followed by another cheer of spontaneous friendliness.

Through a fading March afternoon the party returned to Boston and arrived in the city in time to rest before an early dinner, after which they boarded their train for the south.

14: The City of Decision

Next day, at Washington, reporters were waiting once again. Here, in particular, anything pertaining to Hawaii was news. For in this city—soon or late, for good or for ill—an ultimate decision as to that little country's fate was to be made.

Exactly at noon, Kaiulani stepped down before the Arlington Hotel, dressed in a smart navy-blue traveling costume, plumed hat, jacket, and boa. The carriage which had brought her, along with the three Davieses and Miss Whartoff and her French maid, through the rainy streets from the railroad station was followed by another laden with thirteen trunks and eight bags, all marked with her distinctive VK.

Kawananakoa was waiting at the hotel with a lei of roses. This time she did not feel so strange at seeing him as she had felt in New York. The Davieses greeted the Prince pleasantly. But Kaiulani herself was too aware of his fundamental disapproval of her journey to wish to prolong any public interview. After a few moments of polite conversation, she turned to be escorted to her waiting apartment.

The rooms reserved for the party from England, overlooking Vermont Avenue, were said to be those once occupied by that greatest of French actresses, Madame Sarah Bernhardt, during the most recent of her triumphal tours of America. But any imagined echo of that famous *voix d'or* immediately was drowned in the clamor of newspaper men. Frances Folsom Cleveland, the

111

nation's new and young first lady, was the heroine of the hour. What were the Princess's plans to call upon her?

Kaiulani reminded them gently that she was in America as a private individual and had received no invitation to the White House.

"But you can call on her any time, in an informal way," one reporter protested. "And she is almost sure to be pleased to see you."

"I could not do that," Kaiulani chided. "It is not customary. No one would call on a private lady with whom they were not acquainted, as you say, informally. And I do not think that the public station of President Cleveland makes any difference."

In the small silence which followed this soft reproof, Mr. Davies's firm voice addressing other reporters seemed to fill the room:

"Over Wormley's Hotel, where the provisional government commissioners are stopping, I noticed this morning, gentlemen, that the Hawaiian flag is flown. Yet I am told that the *American* flag flies over the Honolulu government buildings. A curious state of affairs!"

Mr. and Mrs. Davies and Kaiulani spent the remainder of the day quietly in their rooms, but at half past eight dined publicly in the hotel dining room, in evening dress—Kaiulani's a trailing black silk skirt and pale yellow bodice, its collar fastened with a diamond crescent. Every head turned as they passed among the tables. A reporter from the *Star* bobbed up in their path, and Mr. Davies presented him. Kaiulani smiled and shook hands, as the delighted newsman told his readers, "in the old-fashioned way, not with the high-elbow jerk that would-be fashionables are using."

Next morning, rain was still falling. But inside the hotel, the weather was forgotten in the pleasure of a private concert presented only for Kaiulani and her companions by the famed violinist Ede Remenyi, who had been entertained by the Cleghorns in Honolulu. The rest of the morning hours were barely long enough for a perusal of the newspapers. The Davies party's arrival was reported in detail, with mentions made of Kaiulani's "shapely white hands, with many rings," and the way she wore her hair "in fluffy bangs, with a high twisted knot." But quite overshadowing such trivia was a truly important story: "President Cleveland this morning sent to the Senate a message withdrawing the Hawaiian treaty which was pending."

This unexpected move had exploded a bombshell on Capitol Hill. Senators who were interviewed by the press were at odds in their explanations. Some believed the pending document to arrange Hawaii's annexation was in opposition to the new Chief Executive's policies. Others argued that Mr. Cleveland merely intended to make a few changes in terms.

Not surprisingly, the brief meeting between Koa and Kaiulani was considered to have romantic implications. One story described them at length (if not with precise accuracy) as: "royal lovers. That is, they were expected to be. And if the course of royal love had gone smoothly with other royal affairs in Hawaii, the Prince was perfectly willing to . . . become the husband of the Princess." (Willing, indeed!)

Another account of their "love affair" had been gleaned from an interview with Doctor Mott-Smith. The ex-Hawaiian Minister reportedly had stated that, until the recent overthrow, Queen Liliuokalani had intended to celebrate their wedding as soon as Kaiulani came of age. "It is said, however, that the Princess has different ideas . . . and that if she has her own way she will marry some young Englishman. It is said that Princess regards herself as being better than the Prince and she will never consent to a union with a native Hawaiian." This was patently another effort to drive a wedge between the throne and a loyal native population! Falsehoods carefully wrapped in "it is said"!

Kaiulani spent the afternoon sight-seeing about the city, while Mr. Davies presented several letters of introduction he had brought to Washington. By evening, the brief public flurry caused by their arrival seemed to be dying down. After all, there was almost a surfeit of Hawaiian visitors in the Capital these days.

Next morning, a trio of gentlemen from the World's Fair Commission called to pay respects and extend to Kaiulani a special invitation for her to visit Chicago during the coming fair. She thanked the Commissioners gracefully, expressing hope that their invitation might be accepted.

For a few days, reporters had to manufacture news about visiting royalty. They wrote that whenever Kaiulani passed through the hotel dining rooms "comments of admiration are heard on all sides." They wrote that Prince David, escorted to inspect the luxurious new coaches of the Pennsylvania Railroad's latest de luxe train, "snuggled down into a leather seat and said, 'After a while the Americans will have theatrical entertainments in their cars!' "

Still pressed about his plans for his ward, Mr. Davies was cornered to make another statement. He told reporters, "I am well aware, gentlemen, that the representatives of the Princess have no diplomatic standing in the United States. Her visit to the President, if one is made, will be purely a social one."

But on March 13 there was real news aplenty. The morning papers reported that President Cleveland had announced he would send a personal commission to Hawaii for a thorough investigation of the rights and wrongs of the overthrow. Only then would his administration commit itself, pro or con, as to annexation of the Islands. This was an obvious blow to the provisional government, whose agents had been laboring so diligently to rush through an annexation bill. Calm consideration of the justice of their demands was the last thing they wanted.

If the prospect of a presidential investigation was one straw to show how the wind was blowing, another was the arrival at the Arlington of a formal invitation for Kaiulani to be "received" at the White House on the same afternoon. Well aware that much might hinge upon the personal impression she created, she dressed for the great event in the most elaborate afternoon costume from any of those thirteen trunks. It was a long-sleeved gown with a flounced skirt and a snugly fitted bodice, and with it she wore her immense new hat in the Gainsborough style trimmed with a rippling forest of ostrich plumes.

Promptly at the fashionable hour of half-past five, she and the Davies family and Miss Whartoff stepped down from their carriage and were shown inside the famous Blue Room. Although there had been careful avoidance of any recognition of politics in the invitation, she was received as a Princess. The smiling woman who had married Mr. Cleveland during his original term as President turned radiantly to greet her—and from that moment, Kaiulani shared warmly in America's universal near-worship for "the White House bride."

The bulky President himself, his lovely wife's senior by a quarter of a century, was more reserved. But he did seem intent upon conveying to Kaiulani (without once introducing the forbidden subject) that he meant to see justice done both to her and to her country, whatever justice might turn out to be. And she (just as carefully skirting all mention of politics) was equally intent upon convincing him that Hawaii's alii were not the undisciplined savages their detractors had pictured. Delighting in his skill as a mimic, she was reminded that the celebrated actor, Mr. Joseph Jefferson, had once said Grover Cleveland missed his calling in taking up law instead of the stage.

Although warmly cordial on both sides, the call was properly brief. When Kaiulani arrived back at the Arlington, the reporters were waiting.

"I was simply infatuated with Mrs. Cleveland," she told them. "She is very beautiful—but all beautiful women are not sweet, you know. But Mrs. Cleveland is both, and I have fallen in love with her. . . . Mr. Cleveland, too, was very entertaining."

Reaction to the proposed commission to Hawaii continued to monopolize public attention. It was reported from San Francisco that the revenue cutter *Rush* was standing by at her moorings, provisioned for a two-months' Pacific cruise. Did the President intend to name his investigators at once? Congressmen and senators bickered, some approving, some protesting. In New York the papers might be filled with details of the formal opening of the grand new Waldorf Hotel with a brilliant charity ball; but here in Washington, Hawaii's fate held the spotlight.

On March 15 Mr. Davies gave a public address on the Hawaiian situation. With typical fair-mindedness, he told his listeners of his personal regard for many of his most determined opponents.

"One of the saddest features of this matter," he said, "is that it has been presented as a plot and a conspiracy of bad men. It is not that. It is the blunder of good men, men to many of whom I would entrust my dearest interests. They have been goaded on by misrule into injustice, forgetting that injustice is no remedy for misrule. Today the provisional government of Hawaii dares not appeal to the electorate to ratify any one of their acts. What kind of government is that?"

On the other side of the fence, Mr. Thurston had come out with an article in the March issue of *North American Review* which stated, "American property interests in Hawaii have become so great that it is no longer a simple matter of political advantage to the United States, or of charity or justice to a weaker neighbor. . . ." And in the *Forum,* Captain Alfred Mahan, stating the viewpoint of a naval strategist on "Hawaii and Our Future Sea Power," made a strong plea for annexing the Islands as a citadel guarding one entrance to the proposed Isthmian Canal connecting the Atlantic and Pacific Oceans, which some said would soon be built in Nicaragua and others in Panama.

Guesses as to whom Mr. Cleveland might name to investigate the situation in Honolulu ended abruptly with the announcement that one man had been given the full responsibility. He was ex-Congressman James H. Blount of Georgia, a man of such integrity that even the opposition could not object. He was already on his way to board the *Rush* in California. Because it was reported that Mr. Cleveland had given his emissary authority paramount over that of all other American officials he might meet, including the bellicose Minister Stevens, he immediately became known as "Paramount" Blount.

With Blount's appointment, pleas and protests from either side of the Hawaiian controversy were futile. The Davies party could only work to improve an already favorable public impression, and thus strike indirectly for Hawaiian independence. On one of the final days of her American visit, Kaiulani and her party were entertained at a luncheon aboard the receiving ship *Dale,* stationed at the Washington Navy Yard. The guests assembled were people prominent enough to lend the Hawaiian cause much support, if their sympathies could be enlisted. Kaiulani did her smiling best to see that they were.

On another evening, a dinner was given by ex-Senator and Mrs. J. B. Henderson, at which Kaiulani's attentive partner was the French ambassador to Washington. It was an excellent opportunity to win over at least one representative of a major European power. On still another occasion, Kaiulani was guest of honor at a reception of the Women's Suffrage Association in the parlors of the Wimodaughsis Club. Either far too many cards had been issued for this occasion, or interest in the royal guest had prompted an unusual number of people to come uninvited; before the evening was well under way, the young man on duty at the door had abandoned his hopeless efforts to admit only those with proper credentials. A frantic message was telephoned to the police, asking help in keeping out the crowds. Since this occasion assumed political significance by the mere fact of its sponsorship, Mr. Davies felt it proper to deliver a short address on the political situation in Hawaii; and it was obvious that his forthright remarks were well received.

From this affair, Kaiulani went on with the Davies and her chaperone to what was probably the most distinguished gathering of their visit—a great reception given in the rooms of the Arlington by the National Geographic Society. At about half-past ten they were escorted into the well-filled parlors by the society's president, Mr. Gardner Hubbard. Among the guests she met half the true powers on Capitol Hill, and worked conscientiously (if indirectly) to win them to Auntie's cause. A mandolin club played sprightly music in the background. There was no sign in all the brilliant gathering of the socially ignored "P.G.s."

With the *Rush* Honolulu-bound, with "Paramount" Blount aboard her, all that could be accomplished at this time in behalf of tiny Hawaii's independence had been accomplished. On March 18, a Saturday, Kaiulani and the loyal Davieses returned to New York and the Brevoort House, to allow themselves a few days of rest before embarking for England.

"We have accomplished all that we had hoped for," Mr. Davies assured the press. "We feel sure there will be no undue haste now, and that the United States will act in a manner in accord with its position among nations."

It was evident that the Washington visit had been a great success, within the limits of political possibility. The P.G.s now were having to hint in the papers that "It might be that Kaiulani would rather be in society in this country than a Queen in Hawaii . . . ," by their own words indicating that America had come to care about her personal future.

Two days before they were to sail, Kaiulani issued a prepared farewell to her new-found American friends through the assembled reporters.

"Before I leave the land," she told them, "I want to thank all whose kindnesses have made my visit such a happy one. Not only the hundreds of hands I have clasped nor the kind smiles I have seen, but the written words of sympathy that have been sent to me from so many homes, has made me feel that whatever happens to me I shall never be a stranger to you again. It was to the American people I spoke and they heard me as I knew they would. And now God bless you for it—from the beautiful home where your fair First Lady reigns to the little crippled boy who sent his loving letter and prayer. . . ."

Mr. Davies announced that his ward would now remain in England for an indefinite period, and would not return to the United States to complete her education. In answer to a question about any possibility of the Princess's mounting the throne during her deposed Aunt's lifetime—"Gentlemen," he said, "the position of Queen of Hawaii is not an attractive one. I would not want her lot"—this with a fond glance toward Kaiulani and Alice —"to fall to one of my daughters."

Almost before this final interview could reach the readers for whom it had been written, the *Majestic* had sailed.

15: Romances and Republics

Following them to England soon came reports of "Paramount" Blount's arrival in Honolulu. The annexationists had turned out in force to welcome him. But he had refused all their offers of hospitality and was maintaining absolute impartiality while he went about his business. Delighted, Auntie wrote, "In this I recognize the high sense of justice and honor in the person who is ruler of the American nation."

In mid-April the *Advertiser* published a story about Kaiulani herself that was, to say the least, exaggerated. It informed its readers that, "the ex-Princess Kaiulani is really engaged to be married to a son of Theo. H. Davies. The young gentleman in question, Mr. Clive Davies, is now studying . . . at Boston. It is stated that he admits . . . his betrothal with the ex-Princess. It is well known that Kaiulani was often a guest of Mr. Davies in his home in Southport, England, and the . . . prospect of the union would account in some measure for the extraordinary zeal lately displayed by Mr. Davies on behalf of the ex-Princess. . . ."

Reports from home indicated that this "engagement" was widely credited. People there were familiarly referring to Clive as "Mr. Kaiulani." At Ainahau, Papa kept busy issuing denials. ("There is not a word of truth in it! It is absurd!") But the rumors refused to die.

Other rumors, too, made April dramatic. Since the end of

119

February, the cruiser *Naniwa*—one of the most powerful ships of the Imperial Japanese Navy—had been lying at anchor off Honolulu. It became known that young Prince Komatsu, thought to be the youth with whom Papa Moi once had suggested Kaiulani's betrothal, was on board. The pro-annexation newspapers suddenly (and almost hysterically) reported that the *Naniwa* carried guns enough to equip three thousand men; and that fifteen hundred Japanese field hands, imported so eagerly a few years back, had undergone Japanese army training before going to Hawaii. The P.G.s claimed that only the American flag floating over their Government Building—that flag immediately hauled down by Mr. Blount's order, once he had learned the dubious circumstances under which it had been raised—had prevented a show of armed might on the part of the Mikado.

As that spring of 1893 drew itself out, Kaiulani for the first time in her life was feeling a financial pinch. The monarchy's overthrow had created havoc with Cleghorn money matters. Her personal allowance, which had to cover everything except food and lodging, had been cut to a mere five hundred dollars a year. To economize, Kaiulani moved from Brighton to what she wrote Auntie was "a dear little home," The Yews, at Burton Latimer, Kettering. Kettering was not far from Great Harrowden Hall, and her former head mistress, Mrs. Sharp, who had given up the school two years earlier, made her one-time pupil welcome here.

"I am as happy as I can possibly be, under the circumstances," Kaiulani wrote to the Queen. "I do a great deal of hard reading, practicing, sewing and gardening. I am getting to be quite a good needle-woman. . . . I will try to be cheerful but I am so homesick! . . ."

Rumors and counter-rumors still circulated about plans to establish a regency for Kaiulani's immediate accession to the toppled throne. Her aunt must have given this gossip very serious consideration, for she wrote at last to Kaiulani directly inquiring into the matter.

"I have never received any proposal from anybody to take the throne," the answer went back in mid-June. "I have not received a word of any sort from anyone except my Father. I am glad that

I am able to say that I have not written to anyone about politics. I have been perfectly miserable during the past four months. I have looked forward to '93 as being the end of my exile. I have considered the four years I have been in England as years of exile. Now it seems as though things would never settle, and I am simply longing to see you all. . . ."

The Davieses had leased a house for the summer in Ireland, at Killiney, a seaside place several miles south of Dublin. They filled it with a house party of sixteen, Kaiulani included. The scenery about Killiney was wildly beautiful, and that lying a few miles inland even more so. A handsome landau and a spirited team of horses made drives through this natural loveliness almost a daily routine. Tennis, the popular amusement of the neighborhood, was played morning, noon, and night by the younger crowd who swept up Kaiulani in their carefree whirl.

There were so many boys in the group that it was no task at all to assemble two elevens for cricket. Picnic lunches and teas were eaten on the ground after the fashion of Hawaiian luaus. Tea at these outings was brewed from water boiled in the woods, which sometimes was so smoky that it was hard to swallow—but which nonetheless added greatly to the adventure of the occasion.

Kaiulani could have been almost happy at Killiney, had it not been for the continuing suspense about affairs at home. Papa wrote that the Queen was a virtual recluse at Washington Place. But Central Union Church stood so near that from its spire enemies could watch her through binoculars. Kaiulani wrote indignantly, "How you must long to go away to some other place! If I were in your place I am afraid I should pine away and die. I could not stand it—I am so tired of waiting."

In the United States some newspapers had excoriated Mr. Cleveland because "native rule, ignorant, naked, heathen, is reestablished; and the dream of an American Republic at the Crossroads of the Pacific . . . has been shattered by Grover Cleveland." Other American journals were equally firm in approval. The venerated New York *Times,* in an article titled "To Convey a Stolen Kingdom," said, "In point of fact, it [the offer of Hawaiian sovereignty by P.G. spokesmen] is a proposition to convey and make over to the United States a stolen kingdom, and the Government of this Republic cannot put itself in the position of a receiver of stolen goods. . . . When it [the Provisional Government] shows title in the consent of the governed, it will be time enough for the United States to negotiate with it. . . ."

Back again at The Yews after the holiday in Ireland, Kaiulani actually looked forward to winter. Mrs. Davies had arranged that she was to spend the season at Wiesbaden, one of five young ladies to be chaperoned to Germany to learn the country's language on home ground. Alice was to be another of the five, so Kaiulani would not feel too lonely.

Sadness touched that early autumn with news of the death of her good friend Sir William Wiseman. In late September she visited the gentle little widow at Priory Rittle. Sir William's name was never directly spoken during that visit. Lady Wiseman's whole thought now seemed to focus upon a proper upbringing for her eight-year-old son, the new baronet, an extraordinarily attractive little boy who adored his mother. At Chelmsford, Kaiulani felt safe among friends. But her stay was, inevitably, a very quiet and subdued interlude.

More stimulating was the week she spent in London as the guest of Mr. and Mrs. Matthew Makalua from home. Here, for a few days, she felt almost personally in touch with the affairs of Honolulu. Another guest was Mr. Hugh Playfair, just returned from visiting the Islands, where he had been presented to Auntie. His account of the ex-Queen's public mistreatment by the P.G.s made Kaiulani's blood boil.

Among the news clippings forwarded from home was one indicating that her eighteenth birthday had not passed unnoticed in the Islands, where earlier birthdays had been public events. The *Advertiser* had noted that in Kaiulani's honor "Yesterday . . . a luau and hookupu were given by the ex-Queen at Washington Place on Beretania Street. A greater number of people stood around outside the grounds than were inside. The national band played all afternoon in a lanai . . . built for the occasion."

At last the Blount Report was back in Washington for President Cleveland's consideration! The conscientious commissioner had determined that no single leader among those haoles now in power, thanks to American arms, would dare risk putting continuance of the provisional government to a popular vote. He noted the highly improper conduct of Minister Stevens in forcibly overthrowing a friendly government. His conclusion was that there existed no tenable grounds, moral or legal, upon which Hawaii could be annexed to the United States.

By the time President Cleveland could act upon this report—sending out as his new Minister to Honolulu, the Honorable Albert S. Willis, with instructions to effect the prompt restoration of the Queen—Kaiulani was about to embark for Germany.

The German winter was an almost altogether pleasant interlude, thanks to this tacit promise of better days ahead. She found the Germans anxious to greet her with every possible kindness; their loyalty to their own Kaiser making them highly sympathetic to the present tribulations of little Hawaii's royal family. The quiet months at Weisbaden, spent chiefly in study, were given a fillip by the attentions of a wealthy *Graf* who came to the point of offering his aristocratic hand in marriage. Although she did not return his devotion, it would have been untrue to say that Kaiulani did not temporarily enjoy it.

Even in Germany, there were rumors from Hawaii. The Blount Report had not dislodged the P.G.s from Iolani Palace. The building was said to have been ransacked by its new tenants, despite all protests from the helpless natives. The great gilt mirrors from the throne room nowadays reflected certain P.G. parlors about Honolulu. The national insignia had been pried loose from the four great iron gates and taken as souvenirs. Children of the P.G.s were even reported to be using royal stationery for their school homework.

The new government had created a mouthpiece newspaper called the *Star,* edited by a respected Honolulu physician, Dr. J. S. McGrew, who was an ardent advocate of annexation. In February the *Star* alarmed readers with a report that Theophilus

Davies was actively recruiting volunteers in Vancouver for the purpose of invading Hawaii and restoring the Queen's power. Mr. Davies had to deny the harebrained scheme.

Studies at Weisbaden were rewarded by a month of pleasures in a less academic world. Taken to Berlin to witness the Grand Parade before the Emperor and Empress, a march of over twenty thousand magnificently uniformed soldiers, the young ladies then were chaperoned to Potsdam, where the Emperor resided when near his capital. It was a beautifully forested spot on the borders of two lakes, made more exciting for young feminine visitors by the fact that the crack regiments were stationed in the neighborhood. There was no lack of handsome officers. Berlin Kaiulani thought a most beautiful city, even more handsome than London, with its squares, small but exquisite parks, and residences.

By the time of her return to England, the spring of 1894 was half over—and the bright hopes of the autumn considerably dimmed. The Honolulu mission of Mr. Willis had run into difficulties. The provisional government (recently so servile in its petitions for annexation) now was howling down the sky with rage at the suggestion that it abdicate; protesting that Grover Cleveland was meddling in the domestic problems of a sovereign state. Without importing American guns to fire upon other Americans, Mr. Cleveland could not budge the P.G.s. And such force of arms would require the unlikely consent of the American Congress.

The Queen, however, had another arrow in her quiver. Japan would not feel the same compunction about a use of force against bandits. And the P.G.s, knowing this, were not likely to defy the Mikado.

In temporary London residence at 10 Beaumont Street, Kaiulani long and earnestly deliberated certain solemn proposals in Auntie's latest letter. At last, in June, she knew what her answer must be:

> I have thought over what you said . . . about my marrying some Prince of Japan. Unless it is absolutely necessary I would rather not do so.
> I could have married an enormously rich German Count, but

I could not care for him. I feel it would be wrong if I married a man I did not love, I should be perfectly unhappy, and . . . instead of being an example to the married women of today, I should become one like them—merely a woman of fashion and most likely a flirt.

For a second summer, Mr. Davies had leased the house at Killiney. Again, Kaiulani was invited to accompany his family to Ireland. The beautiful Irish scenery and the warm welcome of the "county" families now seemed the more pleasant because they were old friends. The tennis and the parties were taken up anew. Yet not even Ireland was free of dark shadows for Kaiulani. It was a dreadful blow to hear from Honolulu that on July 4 a Republic of Hawaii had been proclaimed in Honolulu. The oligarchy there were scrambling to cement their position, in rank defiance of President Cleveland's firm avowal that it was untenable.

A republic was supposed to be a government in the free tradition of the United States of America. Nothing could have been further from fact in Hawaii, no matter what its new masters called themselves.

The convention they had assembled to set up their "Republic" (until some new chance of annexation to the United States, which was a lost cause while Grover Cleveland occupied the White House) had been a travesty of the democratic process. Its "election" was held under voting rules so stringently reserving the franchise to the P.G.s themselves that fewer than eight hundred votes could be cast! On the very holiday celebrated in their homeland as the birthday of liberty and independence, the *haoles* had set up their new Republic by fiat—with much-respected Sanford B. Dole as its first President.

The Davieses had asked Kaiulani to remain as their guest until after Christmas. Waiting for news all through that long Irish summer, she was stunned to learn that the flimsy Republic of Hawaii had received formal recognition by the United States on August 27. Poor Mr. Cleveland had appealed to his Congress for a solution to the Hawaiian problem "which is consistent with . . . honor, integrity and morality." But the Congressmen had bowed to political pressure and granted the usurpers in Honolulu an all-too-hasty endorsement as a legal government.

Distressing developments at home were reported in every new mail. Natives were being threatened with eviction from their homestead plots unless they signed an oath of allegiance to the Republic. One of "Uncle John" Cummins's luaus was invaded and the guests bullied, on the pretext that it was a monarchical gathering. The Hawaiians were forbidden to congregate in large groups, their "democratic" masters being too fearful of outbursts of mass opposition.

Even when the Queen donated a plot of her own private lands in Pauoa Valley for a public park, the government banned general attendance at the dedication ceremonies. But small groups had drifted, one by one and seemingly at random, up nearby hillsides to look on from a distance. And Kawananakoa, officiating, had planted a young *lehua* tree. Every proud, helpless Hawaiian on the surrounding slopes had known that it was Liluokalani's private symbol, and that the young Prince so carefully scrutinized by the suspicious haoles around him was publicly blessing her.

Hearing such reports, it was easy for Kaiulani to recall writings of the poet Goethe studied at Weisbaden, and how he had said (as if of poor Hawaii):

> Not helpless against empery of right
> Has Nature left the weak; she giveth craft
> And pleasure in its use. She teacheth arts—
> To seem to yield, delay and circumvent;
> Brute force deserves to have such weapons used.

When autumn came they returned to Sundown, the Davies place in Southport. Home from his studies in Boston, Clive was there and helping his father with the family's complex business affairs. Kaiulani took her own place in the life of the household, accepting an invitation to participate in a bazaar to aid the Southport Infirmary.

This gala lasted from November 13 through 17. The young ladies working at the particular stall to which Kaiulani was assigned were outfitted in the blue serge dresses, white caps, aprons, collars, and cuffs which were the nursing uniform for the sponsoring St. John Ambulance. During the week of the bazaar, Kaiulani won three separate raffles; the prize for one of them being a lumbering pure-bred St. Bernard dog. This great, clumsy creature was so companionable that she instantly began planning to take him along with her on a coming three-months' visit to Jersey.

On the twenty-third of November, Alice Davies came of age. During their long friendship, Kaiulani had minimized the two years' difference between their ages with laughing reminders that Alice was still an "infant" in the eyes of the law. Now, suddenly, she herself was the only "child" left at Sundown. But how very old and tired a child!

At this strange year's end, she selected a Christmas card for Auntie more carefully than usual. It was tied with yellow ribbons and had a border of forget-me-nots and a white satin insert picturing two robins on a branch of white flowers. The verse was appropriate, considering Auntie's woes:

> I do not bid the bells to ring
> A merry chime of earthly bliss,
> I do not pray that life may pour
> Its so-called blessings in thy way,
> But simply this
> To thee I sing,
> That He whose birth we keep today
> May bless and keep thee evermore.

This was the sixth Christmas she had spent away from home. It sometimes seemed as though she were fated never to go back to Ainahau. When she had made the crossing to Jersey and Mrs. Rooke's beloved house there, her surroundings brought Hawaii to mind even more sharply than they had during her first visit. This island was so small, so inescapably girt with blue sea. But alas for the differences!

Here, soil was so rich that three acres could support a farmer. The barren homestead *kuleanas* of her own people offered only meager returns for hard labor. All the good agricultural land had been pre-empted by the big haole sugar plantations. Yet even their arid farmlets were to be taken away from the Hawaiians, it seemed, unless they betrayed their own hearts and took an oath to those who had unthroned their Queen.

She discovered again the beauties of Jersey's precipitous cliffs. She explored the lanes which meandered past peaceful farmhouses or skirted meadows and grazing fields. The roads leading to the sea were narrow and steep. She tried bicycling, which had become the fashion, but soon learned that Jersey's downward hills were almost too adventuresome, and the upward hills exhausting to pedal.

Still, as winter drew out, she did not abandon her expeditions. She grew to love the sturdy beauty of thornbushes gnarled and stunted by winds that beat across the island's northern shore. On her bicycle she could leave St. Helier and within twenty minutes be in a world of unpeopled hillsides, almost secret valleys, and towering sea cliffs that wore their heather like wild crowns.

January was almost over before she learned of happenings in Hawaii which had ushered in the new year of 1895 with violence and bloodshed. Goaded at last past their ability to endure more, the natives had struck back—with the help of anti-annexationist haoles—at the usurpers of their homeland. They had sailed in a shipload of arms from California and buried them in the sand near Diamond Head to await an hour when their blow for freedom might be struck.

On January 6, a Sunday, the patriots led by a fiery young half-Hawaiian named Robert W. Wilcox and by Captain Samuel Nowlein (lately, commander of Auntie's guard) had begun to gather at the home of lawyer Anton Rosa, out near Diamond Head. The plan had been that early Monday morning they would move on the city, joining supporters awaiting them there. But enthusiastic volunteers soon mixed too much whisky with their high aims. Premature gunfire had brought an alerted haole force out to Waikiki to investigate.

All Sunday night and into Monday, the city had given way to near hysteria. The Republic had mounted a howitzer on the deck of its government tug *Eleu* and shelled the Patriots from the sea, putting them to flight up the valleys. Captain Nowlein's men were surrounded on the Punchbowl heights and pounded into submission. The desperate, heroic bid for freedom was methodically shattered, and its participants herded into the Republic's jails. Their brief, tortured rebellion was over.

Among the two hundred or more prisoners now held were Koa and Kuhio. Auntie herself had been arrested on January 16 and marched to her former palace with only one attendant; there she began what was to turn out to be nine weary months under guard.

Without the formality of a search warrant, officials of the Republic meanwhile had ransacked beautiful Washington Place. All Auntie's personal papers were carted off by her enemies. Then a company of the Republic's militia had turned out the mansion from cellar to attic, taking away even dead Uncle John Dominis's personal jewelry.

On January 22, in order to prevent the execution of prisoners whose only fault had been refusal to submit to treason against their Queen, Her Majesty had signed a document prepared by the Republic. It stated that she forever relinquished all claim to the throne of Hawaii.

16: "World Enough, and Time"

Liliuokalani herself was formally charged by the Republic of Hawaii with "misprision of treason"—the claim being made, with no supporting evidence, that she had held prior knowledge of the counter-revolution.

Her trial was begun on February 8, in what once had been her throne room. An obviously biased Military Commission was assembled to hear the case. Their vicious travesty of legality was obviously aimed at humiliating the Queen before the large crowd gathered to listen. But her natural dignity foiled them. One of the chief complaints of reporters covering the trial was that the "haughty" woman had refused to break. Her eventual sentence —the maximum penalty for the crime of which they accused her —was a fine of five thousand dollars and five years' imprisonment at hard labor. But no one meant actually to carry out the harsh judgment. It was merely a whip to terrify the Hawaiians into permanent submission.

Amid such a flow of agonizing news from home, spring began. Poor, poor Auntie! Kaiulani's heart ached for her. By comparison, other Honolulu tidings faded to triviality; even those intimately concerning herself. On May 17, the *Bulletin* carried a full report of her personal estate, on which Papa just had filed a final accounting as trustee. Mama's jewelry received major attention here. The listing of it evidently had dazzled the writer, for he added: "Now that Miss Kaiulani is in lawful and peaceable possession of the above . . . she ought to be satisfied, at least most young ladies would be. If not she will at least be able to open a jewelry store and run in opposition to Tom Lindsay. . . ." (Mr. Lindsay's shop for jewelry and watches, she recalled, was in the Campbell block on Merchant Street.)

But far more precious to Kaiulani than any ring or necklace was the news that Papa himself was coming to Europe again! He would be here by midsummer!

Archibald Cleghorn—so much older looking this time, yet otherwise unchanged—reached England on August 10. He brought, if not happy news, at least a personal and first-hand account of poor Auntie.

Early in June, he told her, whispers had stirred Honolulu that the Republic (having humiliated her to the full extent of its ability) was making ready to release the ex-Queen. But up until his sailing, nothing actually had been done. Though her health was failing in confinement, the Queen still refused her captors' offer of a daily drive outside the palace. The spectacle of her carriage passing under armed guard was one she meant to spare still-loyal hearts that might be bruised by it.

With Papa so wonderfully with her again, Kaiulani saw out the summer's final weeks as guest of the ever-solicitous Davieses. When this visit with their stanchest friends was ended, the two Cleghorns went on to Scotland. Travelers, they were also drifters with time somehow to be put behind them, but with nothing at all definite lying ahead. In this same mood of drifting, they were back in London by November and making preparations to winter on the Riviera.

By then they had been informed that on September 6 Auntie had really won release from her prison at the former palace, although only on parole. Kuhio and others also had been "conditionally pardoned." Auntie's letters (which began arriving again as soon as she was free to write them) told the exiles that she had been forbidden by the Republic to attend any large gatherings, even services at church.

Installed for the season with Papa at Villa Dimure au Cap,

près de Menton, Kaiulani discovered that at least on the Riviera she was still greeted as royalty, still known as the Princess of Hawaii.

Among the international set who made the playground gay were a couple named Kennedy and their grown children, who took particular pains to see that the Cleghorns were amused. An "at home" was held each Thursday at the Kennedy villa, and usually included dancing. The parties were among the brightest in the colony, and the Kennedy kindnesses earned Kaiulani's gratitude.

Nearby, at the Cap Martin Hotel, a woman in whom Kaiulani was deeply interested had installed her retinue for the winter. Elizabeth, Empress of Austria, still seemed shadowed by the tragic six-year-old mystery of her only son Rudolf's death at Mayerling. Her husband, the Emperor Franz Josef, had sat his throne while five Hawaiian monarchs and even their throne itself had vanished into limbo. Yet here was this remarkable Empress, who might be seen daily setting out upon five-hour walks that would have exhausted hikers half her age.

In Christmas week Kaiulani wrote Auntie the most cheerful letter she could devise: "Up to the present time, my Father and I have enjoyed pretty good health. . . . I can hardly realize that next Wednesday is Xmas day, I hope that before another year has passed I shall be able to personally give you my best wishes. . . ." (The old, threadbare hope!)

A year ended. A year began. But 1896 seemed to offer nothing beyond a continuation of the past, except that Auntie wrote she had been released from parole and was quitting Honolulu for Waialua. The Riviera season wore itself out. The fashionables at the Menton hotels and *pensions* departed like migrating birds, and it was April again. Mr. Davies had gone to Honolulu on business, and found local politics there still in so restless a state that he had made another public statement denying Kaiulani's personal political ambitions.

Drifting still, the Cleghorns themselves left the Villa Dimure au Cap in early May and followed the other migrants northward. Three weeks of that month they spent pleasantly, unpurposefully in Paris. It was here that copies of the *Advertiser* for May Day caught up with them.

One story ran:

> The salaries and pay roll appropriation bill has been signed by the President, and the "Monowai" will carry away a letter to Kaiulani containing information that the Government . . . has appropriated for her separate use the sum of two thousand dollars per annum. . . .
>
> The appropriation for her allowance was made without serious objection from members of either the Senate or the House. The only question was regarding her fealty to the Republic, and . . . that was swept aside by letters from Mr. Davies which appeared . . . a few weeks ago.

Tiring of Paris, she and Papa drifted on once more—this time to Jersey. They had decided to spend the summer there, at Rozel. Welcome as even a small pension from the Republic might be financially, it also had the saddening effect of driving a last nail into the coffin of the old Hawaii.

Jersey was perhaps not the best place in which to adjust to this ultimate reality. The tiny island always had been passionately royalist. Since the dim days of King John, it had given England's crown unswerving loyalty—loyalty so firm that Edward II had bestowed upon Jerseymen his own royal seal of three leopards *passant gardant*. On each walk she took with Papa, Kaiulani could look down upon wild little bays where Jerseymen of long ago, after the beheading of King Charles I, had rushed into the sea behind their fiery leader Sir George Carteret, to meet Cromwell's ships as they came. Men without weapons actually had borne their armed comrades on their shoulders, mounting such a defense that the Roundheads were turned back. Hawaii's own latter-day Carterets (Sam Nowlein, Robert Wilcox, Lot Lane) had proven less effective—but no less steadfast!

The Cleghorns remained on Jersey throughout most of the summer, residing quietly among the gnarled, dark farmers and their black-sunbonneted women. Days were spent watching island birds—cormorants, magpies, flocks of starlings. Nights brought no visitors more important than the *crapauds,* those huge but harmless local toads with which every country lane came alive after dark.

At summer's end, Kaiulani and her father crossed the Channel. By September they were embarked upon a new round of visits to friends scattered through England and Scotland. One week they spent as guests of Mr. Bailie Darsie of Anstruther, Fife, and his wife Arii Titua Marama, who had been Tahitian royalty. Kaiulani found a vague comfort in the presence of someone with a background similar to her own, here in Papa's homeland. But Mrs. Darsie's circumstances were, really, so very different.

The aimlessness of their wanderings often brought to mind an old English poem by Andrew Marvell, studied at Great Harrowden Hall, in which the poet sighed, "Had we but world enough, and time . . ." World enough, and time! That was the stuff these long months seemed made of!

Her birthday in October was uneventful, save that she celebrated it in Papa's company. But several weeks later there arrived an Island-printed souvenir, verses by a Frank Godfrey entitled "In Remembrance."

> Well-loved Princess of Hawaii,
>   Wanderer now in Scotland's isle,
> Accept on this, thy natal day,
>   'Membrance dear in thy exile.
>
> Here, beneath blue, tropic skies,
>   On emerald isle, in azure sea,
> Where first ope'd thy lustrous eyes
>   Are many hearts of love for thee.
>
> The cocoa of its crest of spears
>   Stands sentry as in days of yore
> And silver riplets shed their tears
>   Before thy vacant mansion door.
>
> Now spirit voices fill the air
>   And birds and flowers the story know
> Of one who dwelt among them here,
>   A happy princess—long ago.

Those happy days of long ago
Fond memories bring today, *alii,*
A princely home, with cheer aglow,
On your birthdays, at Waikiki.

A votre santé! Fare thee well!
Good angels ever guard thy way.
May foreign welcome greet thee, 'til
God sends thee home, to *Hawaii Nei.*

Far more interesting than another birthday was word from home that she had acquired a new "cousin." On October 8, Kuhio was married to Elizabeth Kahanu Kaauwai, a daughter of one of the chiefly lines on the island of Kauai. Dear Kuhio, a married man! She remembered him fondly—the quietest and most serious of Mama Moi's three nephews. Somehow she would have expected a romance in the family to star the dashing Koa rather than his younger brother. But she wished the bridegroom and his bride a lifetime of happiness, and promptly wrote Kuhio to tell him so.

In London, upon her return there, Kaiulani had been sitting for her portrait by Monsieur du Boismenant. She posed in a yellow ball gown, holding a bouquet of marguerites in her lap. Papa was much pleased with the pastel, which he intended to ship home to Ainahau when it was completed. But various friends who saw it, although they praised it, spoke of the "rather sad expression."

In distant America, the four years of Mr. Cleveland's second term were ending. In a new election the Republican candidate, Mr. William McKinley, had defeated William Jennings Bryan as the succeeding President. Annexationists were said to be jubilant, reviving all their old efforts to make Hawaii a part of the United States.

By December, the Cleghorns were back again at Menton on the Riviera, this time stopping at the Hotel du Louvre. Here they learned that they were not the only travelers in the family. Attended by her secretary, Joseph Heleluhe, Auntie had set out for the United States early in the month. President Dole himself had sent to her ship a passport made out to "Liliuokalani of Hawaii" —an odd, perhaps inadvertent reversion to his early Monarchical training. "And for the first time," Auntie wrote, "I drew a long breath of freedom."

A reporter from *Harper's Bazaar* interviewed the ex-Queen soon after her arrival in America:

> There rises to greet you, with a slow and singular grace which is majesty itself . . . a beautifully gowned woman. . . . Her voice is like music, low, clear, but penetrating . . . her smile most lovely; her large liquid eyes at once soft and brilliant and very beautiful. . . . She is a deeply religious woman . . . and never makes unkind remarks about her enemies individually. . . .

Auntie shone for Kaiulani in the words, alive and real.

17: An End to Waiting

During this second winter on the Riviera, the strain of maintaining herself as the Princess of Hawaii—and in the fashion this international set expected—was increased for Kaiulani by recurring illness. To Auntie (now in Boston, visiting Uncle John Dominis's "Cousin Sara," Mrs. William Lee) she wrote, "I don't feel as strong as I ought to and I fancy it is owing to my having had the grip so often, seven times since I have been abroad. Papa has a bad cold now. . . ."

Even Papa, who seldom discussed finances, was depressed by the mounting costs of their protracted travels. He admitted in one of his letters to Mama's sister that "We are very hard up for money, more so than at any time since we left home." Auntie seemed very far away. Her new personal equerry, Captain Julius Palmer, was their source for news of many of her activities. By February the ex-Queen had reached Washington with her suite. The city was already preparing for the inauguration of President McKinley in March, and Auntie (established at the new Hotel Cairo on "Q" Street) was to attend these ceremonies.

With Her Majesty in America, the Cleghorns still were not cut off from home. Queen Dowager Kapiolani sent a warm letter which arrived in March, written from Kailua. And late in the month, to Kaiulani's anguish and Papa's dismay, came word that her half-sister Annie (only twenty-nine years old!) had died at home on the sixth. It seemed almost impossible that dear Annie was no longer there in Honolulu, awaiting their return.

Plans already made before the arrival of this distressing news were adhered to. Papa's cold had proven so severe that he felt it wise not to travel. But on the second of April, chaperoned by an American lady they had met at Menton, Kaiulani departed for Paris. If the weather proved seasonable, her stay there was to last indefinitely.

In Paris, the social season had not yet commenced. She settled quietly into rooms at 37 Avenue Marceau, Champs Élysées. Almost a month off lay the opening of the *Grande Bazar de Charité* with which the gay city would come to life. She was invited to attend the *Bazar* on its opening afternoon, as the Princess of Hawaii. Erected on property facing the Rue Jean-Goujon, adjoining the Hotel du Palais, the stalls were to represent a street of old Paris. The *Bazar,* to raise funds for the poor, was one of the rare public events in which even the most exclusive set of the Faubourg St. Germain participated.

Letters arrived from Mrs. Davies in England, who was not at all well herself but who had interesting news of Mr. Davies to relate. Among the British Archives in London he just had come upon the original log of the ship *Discovery,* in which Captain James Cook had arrived off Kauai on January 19, 1778, to become the first known white man to set eyes upon the Hawaiian Islands.

Taken after Cook's death to Kamchatka by a Russian man-of-war, and from there to St. Petersburg, the log at some later date had been sent from Russia to London and there had lain forgotten. Together with the log book itself, Mr. Davies had found the diary of one of the young officers of the vessel. Copies of these interesting documents, Mrs. Davies said, were being forwarded to Honolulu.

Europe was restless in this April of 1897. A Greek steamer had been sunk by a Turkish battery at Preveza, the Greek fleet had retaliated, and Turks had captured Milouna Pass in a savage fight. Daily, one read headlines of a war which was the more senseless because only an ancient grudge had caused it. Soon Greek defeats were bringing rioting in Athens.

News from Washington included one trivial yet amusing item. At the request of Cousin Sara Lee, interested in collecting exhibits for an International Doll Show, Auntie had promised to donate a Hawaiian doll. It had been made to resemble a pretty part-haole, part-Polynesian girl. And Auntie, sewing a tiny holoku and fashioning a miniature head wreath and longer neck lei, had christened her contribution "Kaiulani."

A new United States Minister to Hawaii had been named, replacing Mr. Willis. President McKinley's appointee, Mr. Harold M. Sewall, was a ship-builder's son from Maine. Papa's American friends advised him that "the appointment is regarded here as strongly indicating that the policy of the Administration will be to secure the annexation of Hawaii in spite of Secretary [of State] Sherman's strong position against it."

Young Mr. Sewall was believed to be an ardent annexationist. Financially, this was understandable. His colleagues were said to have invested in the Republic of Hawaii's bonds at a heavy discount. Annexation would mean that these securities could be sold at par as obligations of the United States, with handsome profits to the holders.

As planned at Menton, Papa (greatly improved in health) reached Paris before May Day. And now only a few days remained before the anticipated opening of the *Grande Bazar*. Those who had glimpsed the arrangements now all but completed spread word that a charming occasion was in the making. In its cul-de-sac covering almost an acre, hemmed in on three sides by tall buildings, the "street" created by the sponsors had come to quaint life. The pretty mock houses and shops stood in readiness.

But on the long-awaited morning of May 5, Kaiulani awoke with one of those nagging headaches which had plagued her recurrently since the time of Auntie's dethronement. Summoned by Papa, a doctor advised her at noon that she was not to visit the crowded *Bazar* until a later date.

The afternoon was a long, gray endurance of pain and disappointment. From the streets below rose the clop-clop of brisk teams on their way to the gala. It was easy to imagine the rows of fine carriages lining the avenues adjacent to the *Bazar,* while their fashionably gowned passengers hurried toward the waiting enchantments.

A first signal of anything amiss came almost exactly at the hour of four; and it came as a far-away shout which somehow held a note very different from merrymaking. Its quality drew Papa quickly to the window. His instinctive gasp brought Kaiulani up off her couch.

Already, people on the walks below were running in the direction of the streets bordering the *Bazar*—the Avenue Montaigne, the Place Alma, the Rue François. Hurrying down to investigate, Papa soon returned with an explanation. A fire terrible beyond description had broken out at the scene of festivities, originating, it was said, when the illuminating apparatus of a *cinematograph* exploded and ignited Turkish hangings. There had been time only for a wild shout of warning—*"Feu, mesdames! Sortez!"*—before the first telltale flicker became a holocaust.

Five minutes after that first alarm, the flimsy wooden roof—made more flammable by its weather-proofing of tar—had crashed blazing upon a screaming crowd. Children were trapped on the wooden horses of the merry-go-round. Shrieking women, filmy holiday clothing torn or burned from their bodies, had jammed the exits in blind flight. The high walls on three sides had made the *Bazar* a death trap for hundreds.

Nightmare closed in upon the Champs Élysées. Numberless carriages clotted the usually happy thoroughfare, their occupants weeping openly and imploring strangers for news of loved ones. Ambassadors and noblemen hunted side by side with the humblest. More than one of the searchers went insane from the sheer horror of a tragedy which, only through the random accident of a headache, Kaiulani had been spared.

Morning papers reported a heart-rending scene at the Palais d'Industrie, where burned bodies were being taken as soon as recovered. "No painter," it was stated, "ever imagined a Last Judgment so appalling." At the Palais, in a large room to the side flanking the Avenue Danton, three long rows of silent figures lay on sheet-covered planks. Like ghosts, searchers moved among the victims by smoking torchlight—seeking, seeking. When one of the dead was identified, a coffin was brought from a great pile at the room's center. Nuns with hands folded on their breasts accompanied the sobbing relatives.

Paris was in mourning. Bells tolled at Notre Dame, where a mass funeral was arranged. All the brilliant parties were canceled. Theaters closed. The cafés were deserted. Public business was suspended. By the second day, newspapers were proclaiming that the catastrophe "will always be remembered as one of the most fearful that ever befell a European city." On May 9, still dazed at the ghastly fate she herself had escaped by mere chance, Kaiulani wrote to Auntie on the black-banded stationery purchased because of Annie's death:

> I have never heard of anything so fearful in my life. Nearly all the hundred and seventeen victims were women, and young ones too. . . . There is a Count next door who has lost his two daughters, girls of eighteen and nineteen. . . . Just imagine all those people gone in less than half an hour, and the dreadful agony they must have suffered. . . . I have never seen any place so overcast as the gay city of Paris.

Her reaction to the disaster was so marked that *M. le docteur* held a conference with Papa. On the eighteenth of a month which had forgotten all promise of pleasure, she and her father set out for England, for Ravensdale, Tunbridge Wells, and the new home of the loyal Davieses.

The summer was aimless, like the winter and spring which had preceded it. A restful sojourn at Tunbridge Wells was followed by visits in Scotland, among these a second stay with the Darcies; and then by a retreat (for such it seemed) to the healing quiet of Jersey.

June 28's issue of the *Independent* followed them there from Honolulu. A confidential letter written to Washington—unsigned in print, but known to be the work of one of the prominent Americans in the community—had been made public. It carried such a picture of the Republic of Hawaii that one read it amazed:

> I am in no sense a royalist. . . . Rather I would believe in the divine right of the people, that all men are born free and equal. . . . But the incongruous elements that with us form the body politic . . . controlled in the main by a narrow clique aptly designated the Family Compact, whose motto has ever been to ruin where it failed to rule . . . emphasizes the impracticability of so-called republican institutions among us. . . .
>
> Living under a mythical republic composed merely of its office holders . . . a minority upheld by force of arms . . . these are but a few of the factors which have [produced] intense disgust and hostility against the present absurd methods of government. And that is the situation as it exists in Hawaii today; apathy, disgust and hostility.
>
> Now . . . after this, what? There is no standard around which to rally. . . . Give [our] longings and aspirations a concrete form, send for your Kaiulani, let her after a reasonable sojourn among the American people, during which they may discover for themselves her true worth, her fitness for the position of Queen over the Hawaiian people, return to the land of her birth, once more to take up her residence. . . . Not to agitate, or to conspire, or to make deals and combinations with this factor or that, but to quietly and confidently bide the time when the indignant protests of all right-minded, self-respecting citizens against this . . . travesty called a republic shall have swept it out of existence. . . .
>
> I hold that the decision [as to annexation] rests with the Hawaiians; that so long as they, the children of the soil, intelligent citizens, decline to take that view, the United States will take no steps toward Annexation [nor] accede to the ridiculous pretensions of a minority whose motive is . . . merely one of self-interest.
>
> And . . . that is why I am for Kaiulani, and why the slight influence it is my good fortune to be able to wield . . . is cast in her favor, and why the large majority of foreigners—Americans, British, Portuguese—will support the same sentiment at the proper time."

And this was the judgment of one of their own! An American long established in the Islands! One could not but wonder how such firm sentiments might affect the new American minister in Honolulu.

Whatever his views on annexation, there was small doubt of Harold Sewall's complete Americanism. On July 4, following a gala parade, he had given a pro-American address at the Opera House which had been greeted with "an ovation [said the *Star*] such as has never been given to any man here in many years."

The Cleghorns had also Clive Davies' first-hand word of the new minister's popularity. Now living at the family's Oahu mansion, Craigside, and representing his father's business interests in the Islands, Clive reported that the Sewalls were locally held in high esteem.

Suddenly, on June 16, President McKinley submitted to his Senate the Annexation Treaty so desired by the fathers of the Republic. In Washington, the Cleghorns were told, Auntie at once filed formal protest with Secretary of State John Sherman, known to be opposed to taking over the Islands. Joseph Heleluhe at the same time made official remonstrance in the names of the Hawaiian patriotic leagues he represented.

The treaty met with prompt and stubborn opposition on Capitol Hill. Newspapers all over America cried out against it. Supporters rushed to Washington, to Boston, to New York, attempting to rally approval. But the Senate's current session ended without treaty action.

In the quiet of their Channel retreat, Kaiulani and her father gave sober consideration to these events. Certain conclusions seemed inescapable. Whatever their fate, the Hawaiian people soon would stand in need of that "standard around which to rally." Auntie was their lawful Queen. Yet it did seem Kaiulani might now serve her people in a special way.

If the Republic indeed should fall, then someone who had not suffered so deeply as Auntie (and who therefore might be more able to forgive) should be on hand to lead the Hawaiians from thoughts of vengeance. If the Republic continued, the example of one of their *alii* enduring their tribulations with them might be of immeasurable value. And if annexation came, someone ought to help them accept the inevitable.

In all this, Papa agreed. The time had come to end their rootless waiting. They left Jersey for London in mid-September, and made a hasty round of farewell calls. When the *Paris* sailed from Southampton on October 9, bound for New York, they were aboard her.

BOOK III

Princess without a Kingdom

18: "Once More, Dear Home"

Almost the only event to make that voyage of the *Paris* memo-rable was the friendship Kaiulani and her father struck up on shipboard with an attractive thirty-four-year-old Englishman, Mr. Anthony Hope Hawkins. He was better known to the world by the first two of his names, having three years earlier gained a sudden fame as "Anthony Hope," author of a novel called *The Prisoner of Zenda,* which had taken the public by storm. Only this season, Mr. Hawkins had produced a sequel—*Rupert of Hentzau*—which seemed likely to be as popular as its predeces-sor. A reserved yet delightful man, he was excellent company on the crossing.

Puffing tugboats elbowed the liner to her pier, and when the Cleghorn party went down the gangplank they found a carriage waiting. But Papa was delayed in customs, and before Kaiulani and her maid could reach it newsmen had recognized her and swooped. As she could have expected, their questions were chiefly about the political significance of her arrival while the Queen was in Washington still doggedly fighting against the im-pending annexation of her kingdom.

"No political significance whatever," Kaiulani assured them, repeatedly. "I am going to Honolulu to visit old friends." Beyond this, she had only one answer. "You must talk to my father."

While the reporters scribbled their notes, she caught scraps of comment from among them. "Manner affable . . ." "Speaks with frankness . . ." And, more than once, "Tall, slender, Cuban-type beauty . . ." The comparison was puzzling. Why should she be compared to a Cuban?

At last Papa was ready to leave and the livery horses drew their carriage from the pier shed out into windy streets. As they rolled up before the Hotel Albemarle, some time later, a gentleman hurried out to greet them. He proved to be Auntie's secretary, Captain Julius Palmer. Once they had been escorted to their suite, he presented letters from the ex-Queen, a birthday greeting for Kaiulani among them. He told the Cleghorns that Her Majesty had sent him from Washington to welcome them.

They spent the rest of this day, a Saturday, settling themselves at the hotel and recovering land legs after the voyage. Glancing from her windows, Kaiulani could see that many nearby buildings were decked in bunting. Flags flew everywhere. But surely not because the former Princess of Hawaii was passing through the city?

Captain Palmer explained. "The excitement is in honor of Señorita Cisneros, Princess. There is to be a rally for her in Madison Square this evening, after a soiree in the Red Room at Delmonico's."

"Señorita Cisneros?"

The lady's full name, Captain Palmer elaborated, was Evangelina Cosalo y Cisneros, a young Cuban patriot. She had been jailed in her stormy homeland for rather more than merely protesting Spanish tyranny there. Her notion of how to deal with tyrants had included an attempt at assassinating one of her people's hated overlords.

The story of her unlikely arrival in New York was as romantic as any plot by "Anthony Hope." The New York *Journal* had sent down a young reporter named Karl Decker to cover events in Havana. In the best American tradition, Decker had effected the rescue of the Señorita from her dungeon. Bribed jailers and bars sawed from her window had been part of it. She then had been smuggled into the United States, virtually under shot and shell. Tonight, New York welcomed her. Now Kaiulani understood why the reporters had described her as seeming "Cuban." Every young woman with dark hair would be a Cuban, this day.

But deeper comparisons were unavoidable. Here they both were, both bred on tropic islands, and nearly of age. One girl had plotted violence and murder when injustice swamped her land, and now a great city was bursting all bounds to show its enthusiasm. The other girl had silently accepted what must be accepted and resolved to work toward what might be best for her people in a new era. How many New Yorkers even knew this second girl was here among them?

Promptly at eight o'clock that evening, the carriage Papa had rented drove away from the Albemarle. Traffic in the streets already stood almost at a standstill. Flags—Cuba's emblem and the Stars and Stripes alike—flew everywhere. Excitement washed high along the sidewalks.

Well before the Cleghorns had reached Thirty-fourth Street, they were halted altogether. A breathless tension held the crowd, now stretched in unbroken ranks from side to side of Fifth Avenue. Then, from the west, shouts began to rise. A four-horse open carriage was approaching the Avenue. It was surrounded by a guard of honor; swarthy young men in Cuban uniforms, some armed with guns and other with machetes. Behind the carriage marched a battalion of naval cadets.

There were three passengers in the carriage. The elderly lady, who could not be the heroine, must therefore be some sort of duenna; the stalwart young man looked enough like the hero from a story by Mr. Richard Harding Davis to be the *Journal*'s reporter, which cries of recognition from the sidewalks did prove him to be. And between them sat the girl who had chosen the way of violence. She was slim and dark-haired, and tonight for her triumph was wearing white satin, her shoulders protected against the autumn chill by a scarf of dark fur.

The parade passed at a distance from where the Cleghorn carriage was halted. The crowds made way for it, then closed again. In the direction of Delmonico's famous restaurant, new thousands took up the shouting. The Cleghorns' progress toward

Madison Square was slow, but (now that the Señorita had passed by) no longer impossible. As they drew closer to the open area of the park, fireworks were beginning to explode in gaudy designs. Catherine wheels spun. Rockets mounted and arched.

Barely in sight of the square, Kaiulani and her father were halted once more. Here the throngs were packed in close. Every tree bore a fruit of perching figures on its bent branches. Every window framed peering faces. At the foot of General Worth's monument, the Seventh Regiment Band blared patriotic tunes. On a bunting-festooned speakers' stand, from time to time, prominent citizens arose to deliver laudatory orations.

The soiree at Delmonico's must have been brief. The Cleghorns had not waited long before shouts in a side street not far off began to mount into the now-familiar roar. From the corners of the square, four white searchlight beams pounced, converging on a spot just under the platform.

Up into the raw glare of the lights mounted Karl Decker and Evangelina Cosalo y Cisneros. The reporter's arm was flung protectively across the girl's slight shoulders. She seemed to shrink back, head drooping into her furs. But Decker urged her forward.

The square was suddenly as silent as a church. Standing at the edge of the platform, the girl stared out across those thousands of faces. Decker whispered something. She cried, thinly, *"Viva Cuba!"* These two words were all she had to say. At once, they were swallowed up in new roars from the crowd. The people of New York knew her story, and what she had done in the name of liberty spoke for her.

For Kaiulani, that cry of *"Viva Cuba!"* inevitably stirred a softer echo—*"Aloha, Hawaii!"* Would resistance have been a better way than the one she had chosen to show her love for her homeland? Her people were the spawn of warriors. When the blow fell, they had lacked only a strong leader to follow. Had she returned to them then and urged them to it, the streets of Honolulu might have run red. But would violence have improved their future, or have held off for long the sure march of history?

Sunday, and the days following it, were quiet ones at the Albemarle. The city was resting from its wild welcome. Callers came and went at the Cleghorn suite, "Anthony Hope" pleasantly among them. But Papa or Captain Palmer received most of the visitors, answered their questions. No political significance . . . No coolness between the Princess and the ex-Queen . . .

On Tuesday, Kaiulani wrote to Aunt Liliu:

> If quite convenient to you, Papa and I will come down to Washington to pay our respects to you on Thursday. We have found it so difficult arranging our plans . . . and we are having a lot of trouble securing a drawingroom on the train for the west. . . .
>
> Papa sends his love and so do I. I am so looking forward to seeing you. It is such a long time since I had that pleasure. . . .

The Cleghorn party left the Albemarle on Thursday as quietly as they had arrived. And that same afternoon they were in Washington. It would have been unthinkable to leave for home without this brief visit. To all loyal Hawaiians, Auntie was still their Queen. And after all the years that separated them Kaiulani looked forward eagerly to seeing her again.

As she entered the comfortable suite at the Ebbitt House, to which Captain Palmer escorted them, Kaiulani saw an old woman seated behind a writing table near one of the parlor windows. Papers were spread out before her, printed proof-sheets. Captain Palmer had told them that the ex-Queen was at work on a book to be called *Hawaii's Story*, presenting the royal view on all the *haole* revolution.

The woman herself was less easy to recognize than her occupation. Her dark face had aged. The handsome, modish costumes which once had aroused the envy of feminine Honolulu had given way to a *grande dame's* black silks, trim and correct and without a trace of vanity. The mouth—was it possible that carefree laughter had ever stirred that grim mouth?

Liliuokalani rose from her chair and as Kaiulani dipped a deep, reverent curtsey she came around the end of the writing table with her arms flung wide. Graceful still, and firm of step, Mama's sister hurried forward. They embraced each other.

They talked, but most of what they could say to each other— so loving and yet almost strangers—was concerned with yesterdays, to which one could never turn back although once they had seemed destined to endure forever, yesterdays entombed now in the printed galleys of the old Queen's book.

A day or two later, when the brief visit was over, Kaiulani accompanied Papa aboard another train in the Washington station. The width of America now lay ahead of them, and then the homeward voyage of the *Australia*. As the capital city was left behind and rolling fields appeared beyond the car windows, Papa vanished behind his newspaper and snorted as he read. It was easy to guess what annoyed him. The old rumors had been flying anew, and more official denials had been required: "No official action was taken during the meeting of Kaiulani with Her Majesty. The question of politics did not pass their lips."

The alien fields rolled past. Virginia? Maryland? If one were perhaps about to become an American (incredible thought!) then one ought to get the geography straight.

They reached San Francisco so quietly on Tuesday night, October 29, that the *Chronicle* complained, "many persons who were on the same train were not aware of her presence." At the Occidental Hotel, Papa (still anxious to avoid attention) registered them truthfully although misleadingly as "A. S. Cleghorn, daughter and maid, Honolulu."

But by Wednesday evening, reporters were clamoring for interviews. Papa admitted them to their sitting room with one admonition. "My daughter will be pleased to see you, gentlemen. But not to talk politics."

The man from the *Examiner* was particularly impressed by that interview and described her in Thursday's paper with heated denials of the unfavorable rumors some of her aunt's enemies had circulated about her:

> A barbarian princess? Not a bit of it. Not even a hemi-semi-demi barbarian. Rather the very flower—an exotic—of civilization. The Princess Kaiulani is charming, fascinating, individual. She has the taste and style of a French woman; the admirable repose and soft voice of an English woman. She was gowned for dinner in a soft, black, high-necked frock, with the latest Parisian touches in every

fold; a bunch of pink roses in her belt and a slender gold chain around her neck, dangling a lorgnette. She is tall, of willowy slenderness, erect and graceful, with a small, pale face, full red lips, soft expression, dark eyes, a very good nose, and a cloud of crimpy black hair knotted high.

"I shall spend the time here seeing the sights, and with friends," she told the reporters. "I have met a number of our Hawaiian friends already"—she pointed to the baskets and bowls of flowers which had transformed the suite since their arrival— "and, as you know, it is the custom of our people to exchange gifts of flowers." (The *Examiner* man told his readers that "she said 'our people' with a pretty pride and touched the roses at her belt gently.")

Reporting the many parties and entertainments privately arranged for Kaiulani during the few days prior to the *Australia*'s sailing, the *Call* was equally glowing:

> She is beautiful. . . . There is no portrait that does justice to her expressive, small, proud face. She is exquisitely slender and graceful, holds herself like a princess, like a Hawaiian—and I know of no simile more descriptive of grace and dignity than this last. . . . Her accent says London; her figure says New York; her heart says Hawaii. . . . But she is more than a beautiful pretender to an abdicated throne. . . . She has been made a woman of the world by the life she has led. . . ."

One thing Kaiulani found somewhat surprising in San Francisco was the almost universal assumption that she was engaged, or virtually engaged, to marry her distant cousin Prince Kawananakoa.

Koa's personal attractiveness, his almost excessive physical handsomeness, made him an ideal subject for rumors of romance. Kaiulani knew that Papa disapproved of the Prince's numberless love affairs, and that he favored a haole husband for his daughter. Yet against this stood the fact that, next in line after herself, Koa might one day have ruled their homeland as King Kalakaua II. The whole matter made a fertile subject for speculation, and the public had seized upon it happily.

Swiftly and pleasantly though they passed, the San Francisco days were only a time of waiting. When the Golden Gate fell away behind the *Australia* on the following Tuesday, Kaiulani was looking ahead.

The voyage was considerably more enjoyable than it might have been because of the presence on board of Daniel Frawley's theatrical company, on its way to present a dramatic season at the new theater in Honolulu. The actors had made an outstanding Hawaiian success a year earlier, and Kaiulani could guess with what impatience their return must be awaited.

Always chic and gracious, the company's star, Miss Blanche Bates, drew many admiring glances from fellow passengers during the days at sea. But Kaiulani found more interesting a young actress nearer her own age; a girl named Eleanor Robson who was to play lesser roles in the dramas of the company's repertory.

The *Australia* made port on the sunny morning of November 9, having first sighted Molokai's green corduroy-ribbed cliffs as dawn was breaking. Kaiulani was on deck for the long-awaited first glimpse of land, and as Diamond Head rose out of the sea it was impossible not to recall the stirring Pilgrim Chorus of *Tannhäuser,* which she had heard so often in European opera houses during the years on her exile:

> Once more, dear home, I with rapture behold thee,
> And greet the hills that so tenderly fold thee. . . .

The crowd of thousands waiting at the Oceanic wharf, staring out at the approaching ship, was evidence that her people had not forgotten her. High on the hurricane deck, dressed for landing in black skirt and waist of Hawaii's royal yellow, Kaiulani sought to pick out familiar faces. For perhaps a half-hour after the gangplank dropped, she remained on board while welcomers crowded onto the ship to pay their respects. Koa was among them; and Eva Parker, come all the way from the Big Island. When at last the three of them went down with Papa to climb into a landau waiting on the pier, the carnation lei Kaiulani had worn on shipboard was buried under the seeming carriageful of flowers handed up out of the crowd by weeping, smiling well-wishers.

All along the four miles to Waikiki beaming Hawaiians by the road held up their *keikis* to watch the Princess pass. The team turned in at last between gates still marked as she remembered them, *Kapu.* Up the curving carriage road they swept, to halt in the shade of the magnificent old banyan, *her* banyan!

Papa had warned her, of course, that she would find things changed. Nevertheless, she had to look twice to believe it. Save for the banyan, she might not have known Ainahau. The gloomy, comfortable old building she remembered had gone and in its place stood a new and handsome frame structure, two stories high and spreading its wings to either side. The wide lanai which stretched across the front was bathed in sunshine. The house seemed at once very beautiful and very sad—because Papa had built it for a Princess who would no longer need a royal residence.

She hid her emotions as she hurried across the lanai and into the house. An instant later, after crossing an airy hall paved with fancy tiles brought from Chicago, she stood at the entrance to a grand drawing room, a room all too clearly designed for the state receptions of an heiress apparent. About forty feet long and thirty wide, it was lined with long windows which gave out upon velvet-green lawns. Highly polished Island woods had been worked into its paneling. Whatever came now, they were not likely to reflect the soirees of a future queen.

Off one end of this large apartment lay a smaller "mosquito room," its windows reaching from floor to ceiling and shielded by screens and Venetian blinds. Here she and her ladies-in-waiting might have sat, had history not intervened, sewing and chattering the pleasant hours away.

Upstairs, directly above the drawing room, she was shown the suite Papa had built for her private use, with a boudoir opening off one end of the large bedchamber, and a dressing room off the other. In the decoration of the high ceiling, repeated over and over, were the Hawaiian coronet and the kahili—symbols of the royal chiefs.

Last of all, she was taken to the roof, reached from the upper hall by way of a staircase almost as steep as a ladder. Papa mounted almost as lithely as his three younger companions.

Out upon the flat roof, Kaiulani, her father, Eva, and Koa all stood motionless. Acres of rice fields, tenderly green, spread below them. Beyond, the great mountains brooded—perhaps not quite so great, after one had viewed the Alps. Veils of cloud drifted in tattered sweeps across their stark peaks. Far off, the ships in harbor rode sedately.

The air was clear, and full of a rising scent of flowers. Kaiulani took a deep breath and held it, not daring at first to speak. *"This* hasn't changed!" she whispered. "Papa, I'm home!"

Two days later, the *Commercial Advertiser,* which only the morning before had published a harmless account of her homecoming, was back in its role as voice for the Republic's overlords.

"The Washington *Post* claims," it reported breathlessly, "to have abundant evidence of the purpose of Princess Kaiulani to work up a boom to obtain the Hawaiian throne." But the writer was compelled to add, somewhat lamely, "It is said that at present, however, both the ex-Queen and the Princess will not quarrel over the affair. . . ."

The same issue's society notes were less sensational: "Princess Kaiulani is now well established at . . . Waikiki. The Princess had many visitors yesterday, but managed to find time for a trip to the Mausoleum."

The waves of callers had not been half so taxing as that drive up Nuuanu to the spot where Mama—and now Papa Moi, as well—were at rest. Although sunlight was bright at the top of the stone stairs, the royal crypt below had been chilly and the flowers Kaiulani brought had not dispelled its gloom. (But Mama had so loved her flowers, their scent always present as she passed by in her gay laughter or her terrifying rages.)

At the end of the week the stream of people anxious to see her was still crowding the Waikiki road. Some came for love, some from mere curiosity. She received them all, native and haole alike, with quiet courtesy.

Among them, the caller who perhaps interested her most was Kuhio's bride, now Princess Elizabeth. Kaiulani found her new "cousin" to be one of the most impressive Hawaiian women she had seen—a Juno, and regal as a queen, with warm, tawny skin and masses of dark hair in which the sunlight struck bronze glints. Handsomely gowned and jeweled, exquisitely civilized, yet with a hint of something barbaric flashing occasionally in her calm black eyes, Elizabeth was to be a striking addition to the circle at Ainahau.

The Saturday following her homecoming was also the final night of the bicycle-racing season at Cyclomere Park, new rendezvous for Honolulu sport-lovers. Arriving there with a party including Koa and Papa, Kaiulani waited until the crowd's cheers for the winner of the mile open professional race had subsided before making an actual appearance on the track. As she was sighted moving forward on Koa's arm, the band broke spontaneously into the Monarchy's old anthem, "Hawaii Ponoi." The audience surged to its feet as the party passed. Evidently the throne was still remembered!

Those first days following her homecoming were crowded with entertainments. Much later, Mr. Frawley's promising young actress Eleanor Robson would write

> Charming parties were arranged to welcome her [Kaiulani] to which members of the Frawley company were invited. . . . At night, trees festooned with . . . lanterns and aided by Hawaiian moonlight, resembled fairyland. Beautiful dark faces of the natives . . . were framed in every window, smiling as they watched their beloved Princess and the rest of us dancing until dawn and after. . . .

But sometimes, as she tried to meet this gaiety halfway, Kaiulani felt unequal to the task. She wrote to the Queen in Washington:

> Last Sunday the Hawaiians came out to see me. There were several hundreds, and by six o'clock I didn't know what to do with myself, I was so tired. . . . It made me feel so sad to see so many of the Hawaiians looking so poor. In the old days I am sure there were not so many people almost destitute. . . .

I eat poi and raw fish as though I had never left. And I find that I have not forgotten my Hawaiian. . . . I will write again very soon, but at present I feel the heat so much. I can't settle to anything. . . .

19: Miss Cleghorn in Residence

But while Kaiulani might confide her sorrow to Aunt Liliu she could not show it to the world at large. Privacy in their grief was now one of the few things left to the Hawaiians. So Kaiulani patiently discharged the public duties expected of her, such as one day visiting the young pupils at St. Andrew's Priory and another appearing at the Hawaiian Hotel for a concert by Captain Berger's band.

The papers stated that Princess Kaiulani probably would move from Waikiki to Washington Place, as "an accommodation to the people who cannot go as far as Ainahau to call on her." The implication was obvious. A Princess no longer likely to mount her throne was worth just so much *haole* attention, but not one hour's more.

The season was beginning at the fashionable Pacific Tennis Club on Palace Square, and the members invited her to be guest of honor on the afternoon of their first Ladies' Day. When she arrived, accompanied by Papa and Eva Parker, Kaiulani was careful not to glance across at the turrets of Iolani Palace, visible above intervening trees. Secretly, she was determined never again to set foot there now that the proud building no longer housed Hawaiian royalty. She permitted herself to be led to the club's decorated veranda by her waiting escorts. The crowd flocked about them, attentive, solicitous. She smiled and smiled.

On Friday, November 19, came the much-anticipated opening

of Daniel Frawley's theater season. The house had been sold out well in advance, and the newspapers had announced (in hopes, perhaps, of partisan excitement) that American Minister Harold Sewall would occupy the Irwin box at one side of the stage and Princess Kaiulani the lower box opposite. The opening bill was to be a play entitled *Christopher, Junior.* That day, heavy rains turned the unpaved street in front of the new theater into a sea of mud, in which pedestrians found uncertain footing and carriages stalled. But Honolulu would have endured far greater hardships to attend Daniel Frawley's first night.

The new little Opera House received its audience like a duchess in full regalia. Though it was small, its vivid red carpeting and its ornate boxes (including a royal box, never to be occupied except by the former ruler's family and guests) were quite the equal of anything Kaiulani had seen in Europe. The drop curtain was a painting of the Palace of Truth, a palace straight from a fairy tale, with a boat drifting dreamily across its improbable blue lake.

In the Sewall box, with the minister and his wife, sat one present and one former United States senator. Both gentlemen, it was known, were visiting the Islands on business related to possible annexation. Surrounded by loyal women friends, Kaiulani nodded pleasant acknowledgment to Mr. Sewall's bow of greeting, well aware that every eye in the theater was appraising royalty's reaction to the Americans.

It was a bad time in Honolulu for even the memories of royalty. This same week, the official belongings of the late King Kalakaua were sold at auction. The crowd far exceeded expectations and bidding was lively, with wine glasses from the palace sets going at a dollar each and the plates from the dinner service at from six to ten dollars. Mr. Davies paid eight hundred dollars for a pair of the dead King's candelabra. The auctioneer was compelled to close his doors during the afternoon of the sale, to arrange for the delivery of items already disposed of. Smugly, the government could report that it was "well satisfied with the sale to date." Poor Papa Moi!

On one of Kaiulani's first afternoons after she had re-established herself at Ainahau, she went to call upon the Queen Dowager—dear Mama Moi. Since vacating the palace, Kapiolani had retired to her villa at Waikiki, where her nephews Koa and Kuhio lived with her.

A waiting servant took charge of her horses in the driveway and Kaiulani went inside, where another attendant came to greet her, silk holoku rustling, and guided her into the drawing room before hurrying off in search of the old Queen.

It was a comfortable room, oddly mingling objects Hawaiian and alien. Its brown rep suite of furniture had not been fashionable for twenty years. But over one armchair was flung an *ahuula* made of a sea bird's feathers, and at the center of the vast Brussels carpet with its pattern of crimson and yellow roses stood a kahili so huge that its topmost plumes all but touched the ceiling. The walls were literally lined with portraits of Kalakaua, in oil, in crayon, in water color. On an ebony pedestal, to complete the collection, stood his bust in clay.

A tall and commanding figure in a fine black holoku came through an inner doorway—Mama Moi, holding out her ample arms. Despite Kapiolani's advancing age and crippling rheumatism, no gray streaked the hair piled in a lofty coil on top of her head. A lei of *oo* feathers at her neck, the symbol of royalty, was her only ornament other than a gold brooch set with yet another portrait of Kalakaua done in mosaic.

They talked in Hawaiian, since (although she understood the language) the Dowager spoke little English. As she had written to Aunt Liliu, Kaiulani still found herself familiar with her mother's tongue.

Mama Moi readily answered her niece's questions. No, she could not see much hope for Hawaii's future independence, either as a kingdom or as a republic. She supposed that her sister-in-law, in distant Washington, still nurtured such hope. But the annexationists were hard-headed businessmen who must see assurances of success for their cause since they pressed it so determinedly. True, Mr. Cleveland had given the annexationists cold comfort. But Mr. Cleveland was no longer at the helm. Now, Hawaii had Mr. McKinley to deal with.

"*Auwe!*" sighed the old Queen heavily. "Many people called your uncle a wastrel, a lighthead. Yet years ago Kalakaua saw all this coming. Because he did what he could to keep Hawaii for the Hawaiians, the Moi was vilified. Now it is the same with Liliuokalani. But perhaps destiny does not respect mere justice. Events march. The world changes. For myself, I can only pray that God will bring Hawaii a good future. I do not think I ought to tell Him how."

The advice of the Queen Dowager greatly helped Kaiulani to make her own firm decision. For the present and for the immediate future—if not, indeed, forever—the monarchy of Hawaii had ceased to exist. It could do little good to lend herself now to political intrigues. Whether it briefly succeeded or bloodily failed, violence in her name would bring misery upon people who honored her. And this she could not sanction.

Thus committed to herself, she did her best to live quietly as plain Miss Cleghorn of Ainahau. And the last weeks of the year 1897 passed in events trivial enough to fit exactly this retiring role.

The throne's enemies could complain of little except, perhaps, her appearance at one *luau kokua* to benefit charity. Public attendance at this event was so large that carriages blocked all traffic in the neighborhood of Miller and Beretania Streets. The Hawaiian Band played, the lanais and tents were vividly decorated, pretty girls peddled flowers and curios, and one might have assumed it all to be the most innocent of affairs. But the newspapers muttered darkly, "It is said the object of the luau was to obtain funds for the native commissioners in Washington."

If so, the money was well spent. By December 17, reports on that dedicated commission had come back from the American capital. "The anti-Annexation campaign took on new life this evening with the arrival of a commission of native Hawaiians. . . . They lost no time in getting to work from quarters at the Ebbitt House. The great petition they bear, bearing the names of more than half the natives in the Islands, will be presented to the Senate at once."

The paper went on to report "some nervousness" in the annexation camp. It had been discovered that various senators once favoring the taking over of Hawaii now were undecided. The necessary two-thirds Senate vote to ratify the Annexation Treaty did not appear to be forthcoming. Strategy would be altered to push a joint resolution through *both* houses of Congress, where a simple majority could decide it.

With Christmas a scant week away, Kaiulani kept up her decorous appearances in public. She presided over the closing of the fall term at Kawaiahao Seminary, where the young ladies offered a well-attended concert in a hall massed with greens and Hawaiian flags. She attended a special performance at the theater so that she and Papa might be seen sharing the Irwin box with President and Mrs. Dole, in public amity. These small things would be noted and weighed against hotheaded schemes. On the Saturday of Christmas week, a long-time business friend of Papa's, Mr. Monsarrat, gave a luncheon for Kaiulani at Kuliouou, with the Quintette Club playing for dancing. The balls of the season began, and she appeared at each of them—smiling, smiling.

Under this surface there was little except an all-pervading sadness. And her worry for Mama Moi, who had become very ill at her villa. How little this one was truly a Merry Christmas!

Kaiulani and Papa dutifully welcomed 1898 at a ball given by United States Consul General and Mrs. Haywood. More than two hundred people had been invited to dance in the year that well might prove so fateful in Hawaii's history. Admiral Miller, commanding the United States naval vessels then in port, assisted his hosts in receiving. The admiral's band from the *Baltimore* provided tunes to keep the company spinning.

Fifteen numbers had been provided for on the dance cards, the fourteenth—a waltz—to be in progress at the hour of midnight. But the band-leader had miscalculated and the first moment of the new year arrived unexpectedly midway of the thirteenth dance. Instantly, eight bells were struck twice on a ship's bell. The band segued enthusiastically into "The Star-Spangled Banner" not "Hawaii Ponoi," as tact and the actual existence of an independent Republic of Hawaii might have dictated. Beaming haoles exchanged their confident greetings. Kaiulani smiled a polite response whenever one of them turned her way. But anger still burned in her, and dismay, when the evening's final Virginia reel was over and home-bound carriages began to move.

Within two weeks of that party, President Dole had departed for Washington to add his personal prestige to the annexationist artillery already facing indomitable Aunt Liliu there.

Early January was a time of sharp family concern for the Dowager. During the holidays, Mama Moi had taken a turn for the worse, and for two weeks Kaiulani spent most of her days and evenings at the old Queen's villa. Kapiolani had been kept by her doctors from realizing the true gravity of her condition. But one prominent haole lawyer ventured to call with an offer to draw up the royal widow's will. Kaiulani and Koa indignantly refused to grant him an interview with the patient.

"Koa was so mad," she later wrote to Auntie, in Washington, "he gave him to understand that Her Majesty had no desire to make any will, and if she did she had her own lawyer. Did you ever hear such impertinence? He also brought her some cake, but as he did not see her he took it home with him! I admire the haole way of making a present. . . ."

As to rumored "overtures" from the clique in power, she added, "The people of the Govt are not particularly nice to me, excepting Mr. Damon and Mr. Dole. I think they are very sorry to see me here, especially as I give them no cause to complain. Thank God, Annexation is not a fact. The people here are not half so happy as when I first came back. I find everything so much changed. . . ."

On their return to Hawaii Auntie had lent Kaiulani and her father a span of horses which proved "splendid, but a little too full of life for me," and they had been taken back with thanks to Washington Place. To replace them, Papa had purchased a milder pair formerly belonging to the English consul, Mr. Alexander Hawes. In the now more sedately drawn Cleghorn carriage, Kaiulani continued as graciously as she knew how to go to social gatherings. On January 14 she attended a dance aboard the *Bennington*. On the second evening in February she gave a dinner party at Ainahau as a farewell to Clive Davies, bound for England to be married. The days when a sly press had rumored their own engagement seemed far away indeed.

On February 12, the papers reported that Mama Moi had suddenly deeded all her Oahu estates to her two nephews, Koa and Kuhio. Said the story, "The Queen Dowager takes this method of rewarding her nephews for their affection and devotion rather than making a formal will over which there might possibly be some controversy. . . ."

On the fifteenth, returning her compliment to his son, the elder Mr. Davies entertained at Craigside with a card party in Kaiulani's honor. On the nineteenth she went with friends to enjoy the comedies being presented at the Opera House by local casts from the membership of the Kilohana Art League. In both *By Way of a Joke* and *The False Note* tall Andrew Adams played roles which delighted the audience.

This young Englishman, on the staff of the *Advertiser,* was one of Papa's particular favorites. Already Papa had brought him to Ainahau several times, with that special air indicating that Papa expected Kaiulani's approval. Indeed, it would be difficult *not* to approve of Andrew. But what Papa obviously had in mind was another matter entirely; especially now, after she had been so much in Koa's company.

On the week end of Koa's thirtieth birthday, she invited a hundred of their friends to Ainahau for a Saturday afternoon luau. When the feast was over, Koa rose to propose (never more charmingly) the health of their hostess. After this was drunk standing by all the men present, Papa proposed a toast to Koa. Guests lingered on throughout the evening, continuing the celebration—and speculating, perhaps, as to whether or not the occasion might indicate a softening of Archie Cleghorn's opposition to Kaiulani's guessed-at romance with their *bon vivant* Prince.

A few days later, grave news arrived. In the harbor of faraway Havana, Cuba, the American battleship *Maine* had been blown up, supposedly on Spanish orders, and the two powers suddenly growled of war. In American-dominated Honolulu, little else was talked about. "Remember the *Maine!*" was the watchword.

President Dole returned aboard the *Mariposa* on March 4, and the newspapers reported: "Treaty to Wait. Belief That Two-Thirds Vote Is Wanting." With a war threatening America, lesser matters would have to take second place while the Congress coped with immediate emergencies.

By the following Wednesday, copies of Auntie's book on the Hawaiian situation had reached the city, and the haoles were raging at her plain statement of their crimes against her. One pious editorial cried: "If Kalakaua had nominated the Princess Kaiulani as his direct successor, the Monarchy would be in existence today. The love for it was deeply rooted in the hearts of many intelligent and strong men, who winked at its weakness. . . . The Princess has the personal satisfaction of knowing that through no act of hers was the Monarchy terminated." Had the Republic's leaders forgotten so conveniently poor Papa's pleas to them in her behalf? And Mr. Davies's urgent suggestions?

A week later, Mr. Davies and his second son George were to depart for England and the wedding. Kaiulani and Papa sent out invitations to a large farewell reception at Ainahau on the Saturday afternoon. For three hours, the line of arriving and departing carriages was in constant motion. Guests filed past to shake hands with her former guardian and wish him *bon voyage.* "A most delightful function," admitted even the haole newspaper. The surface of things still seemed unruffled.

But the strain of uncertainty was tiring Kaiulani increasingly. On days when public appearances were not required, she strolled the wide lawns, wearing the loose holoku her people favored, weaving leis of green *maile* and feeding the peacocks who strutted with her like cavaliers. One afternoon, a photographer drove out to make an album of views of the gardens authorized by Papa; and he took, among other pictures, two of Kaiulani which showed her, she thought, almost as she really was, tired, unposed, alone in the place she loved best.

The *Commercial Advertiser* soon was printing the claim that

it had in its possession a copy of the report of the recently returned native commissioners to their Aloha Aina society. In spite
of their uniformly good education and high community standing,
these men were solemnly quoted as illiterates: "Queen Liliuokalani want only money. She print a big book to sell for money for
herself. . . . She believe that the United States annex us and
then she have a claim. She want one hundred million dollars.
. . . We do not want her. We want our young Princess. . . . It
is the Princess we will hold out for. . . ." Always the attempt to
sew the seeds of rivalry among Royalists, to divide their loyalty!

Early April's major civic event was a grand concert at the
Opera House to benefit the Kalihi and Moanalua churches. By
eight o'clock, when Kaiulani and her guests arrived in their right-
hand box opposite Mrs. Dole's party, there was not an empty
seat in the house.

The featured singers of the evening were the Kawaihau trio,
who as they took their places on stage bowed first to Kaiulani's
box and then (somewhat less deeply) to the audience in general.
A hush fell as they began their first song—Charles King's new
"Lei No Kaiulani."

> *O ua mau pua lehua*
> *I lawe ia mai no kuu lani*
> *I wili ia me maile lau lii*
> *I ohu i wehi no Kaiulani,*
> *Me he punohu ula ala i ke kai*
> *Ka nohea nohea ke ike aku,*
> *I kuu wehi lani*
> *E ola mau o Kaiuonalani.*
> *E kii mai hoi e lei e Kaiulani e Kaiuoluna*
> *I ko lei lehua puakea*
> *I wiliia me maile laulii. . . ."*

(Bring forth the wreath of *lehua*,
The wreath for our beloved Princess.
Loving hands with the *maile* didst weave
A beautiful crown for Kaiulani.
And upon thy head we will place it,
How lovely and charming to behold there.

Royal and queenly thou art,
Our loving Kaiulani.
This token of love for thee we bring, oh
    receive it, Kaiulani!
Wear your lei of yellow *lehua*
Entwined with the fragrant *maile*. . . .)

When the last note had faded, the audience sprang to its feet clapping and cheering. The trio responded with an encore, and many a native present must have felt his heavy heart lighten as he looked up to where the object of the tribute sat seemingly serene.

The news Honolulu had been awaiting from America came that same week—"War with Spain"!

20: Our Boys in Blue

The Americans were beside themselves in a patriotic frenzy, perhaps some of it genuine, but surely somewhat related to their desire to court the Congress who would decide annexation. When an incoming sail was sighted by Diamond Head Charlie, crowds eager for news raced down to the waterfront. But they learned that the new arrival was a hundred and sixty days out of New York, around the Horn. She had weighed anchor well before the *Maine* even departed for Havana. The excitement at the pier was the crew's first hint that their country was at war.

News did arrive, however, fresh from California. And with it, the general excitement mounted. American troops would shortly be passing through Hawaii on their way to beard the Spaniards in the Philippines! The haoles at once organized a Committee of One Hundred to plan entertainment for these heroes. Here lay their golden opportunity.

The Spanish Consul's protests were ignored. Neutral though she supposedly was, the Republic of Hawaii was throwing open ports and coaling facilities to a fleet that would badly need them. Nothing would be overlooked to prove to Congress that Hawaii was truly American at heart.

At Ainahau, on May 19, Papa wrote the Committee's chairman.

My dear Sir:
I see by the newspapers that it is probable that in a few days a

169

number of officers and men, belonging to the United States Army and Navy, will be passing through Honolulu.

The Princess Kaiulani and I have much pleasure in opening our grounds to them during their stay here between the hours of 9 a.m. and 6 p.m.

With kind regards I am Yours very sincerely,

A. S. Cleghorn

The city grew hysterical with preparations. Ten thousand soldiers coming—that was the generally accepted estimate! "A larger crowd of outsiders than Honolulu has known since Kamehameha and his warriors marched up town from Waikiki," said the delighted prophets of the press.

From Ainahau, on the twenty-fifth, Kaiulani wrote to Auntie, "I am sure you would be disgusted if you could see the way the town is decorated for the American troops. Honolulu is making a fool of itself and I only hope we won't all be ridiculed."

Quite unrelated to the martial excitement of these days was the numbing sadness which settled over the Cleghorn estate when word was received on June 2 from England. Almost without warning, their well-proven friend Theophilus Davies had died there on May 25, where he and George so recently had arrived for the happy family times surrounding Clive's wedding. The realization that she never again would see that stanch, florid face to which she had turned for advice and courage so often, the memories of the man who had stood beside her in England and Washington and Hawaii, engulfed Kaiulani now and stunned her. She was confined to the house at Ainahau, listless with grief.

But outside her father's gates the preparations for the coming troops still held the spotlight. Respected though Mr. Davies had been, his death could not dull the public war fever. Even the Hawaiians, remembering their country's long aloha for America, were joining the haoles in preparations to honor "our boys in blue." It was announced that the Queen Dowager was to present a large silk flag sewn by Hawaiian women to Captain Glass aboard the U.S.S. *Charleston*. But on the appointed day poor Mama Moi was too ill to leave her villa, and Koa and Kuhio had to do the honors in her stead.

The first wave of an approaching tide broke over the eager port during that first week in June. Three steamers were sighted off Oahu's windward coast, and warning was flashed to the city and the fire whistle sounded the signal. The streets promptly erupted in a well-prepared rash of American flags and bunting. The Committee of One Hundred, the National Band, and the officers of the Republic's National Guard all appeared in full regalia, jockeying one another for points of vantage from which to view the approaching transports.

Two of the ships docked that afternoon, the third remaining out in the stream. Troops were not permitted shore leave that night. But the shops in town were stripped by well-wishers eager to send aboard their offerings of tobacco, candy, and fruit. The next day, in two shifts, twenty-four hundred foreign soldiers crowded the streets.

TROOPS IN TOWN! exulted the headlines. HUGE HONOLULU WELCOME! The grounds of the palace built by Papa Moi (but now officially referred to as the Capitol) were thrown open for feeding the visitors. A ton of potato salad, ten thousand ham sandwiches, three hundred gallons of milk, eight hundred watermelons—the list of the food consumed seemed gargantuan.

On the second night after the influx, Koa and Kuhio, maintaining their Islands' reputation for hospitality, gave a luau for the officers of all American vessels in port. When the Republic bade farewell to its enthusiastic guests on Saturday, a careful account of all that had happened was at once sent to the American newspapers.

On the Monday, three hundred of the city's prominent women attended a huge meeting at the Y.W.C.A. to form a Hawaiian Red Cross Society. Naturally, as wife of the United States minister, pretty Mrs. Harold Sewall was named its president. Naturally, as wife of the President of the Republic of Hawaii, Mrs. Sanford Dole was chosen first vice-president. Somewhat less natural, under the circumstances, seemed to Kaiulani her own election as second vice-president. She did not refuse the office, however. Refusal would be the open example of opposition that she did not wish to set her Hawaiians.

And so the pattern of the next several weeks was set. By the end of June, when a second Manila-bound fleet put into port, the Republic of Hawaii had become virtually an outpost of the United States of America.

War fever was the epidemic disease of the Republic, as summer began. On the last Saturday in June, a blue-ribbon meet of star bicycle riders was held at Cyclomere Park to benefit the Red Cross treasury. The boxes and grandstand were crowded to the last seat. At the conclusion of the events, Kaiulani and one of the prominent haole members of the organization decorated the winners with red-white-and-blue rosettes.

That same week end, almost unnoticed, the Queen Dowager filed a petition that the deed transferring her property to her two princely nephews be annulled. A sad family quarrel had ruptured their long-time happy relationship. In the Honolulu of another day, gossip and speculation would have buzzed. But the city's preoccupation with visiting troops at least had the virtue of offering the alii a measure of personal privacy.

One interesting young American who had no official connection with the war arrived in port, during that week, aboard the *Moana*. Mr. Burton Holmes already was a "name" because of his travel lectures illustrated by an amazing new invention which made it possible for pictures to seem to move. His associate, Oscar Bennett de Pue, served as lantern operator and electrical expert for this startling performance, and was indeed the inventor of De Pue's Chronomatographe, the most perfect to that time of all the new so-called "motion-picture" machines.

Applauding everything American, the newspapers were enthusiastic: "Shown will be waterfalls and geysers in action, street scenes where the whole picture is instinct with life, people walking and horses trotting. . . ." These startling educational entertainments began at the Opera House on June 28.

Kaiulani's first glimpse of the noted visitor took place in the surf off Waikiki. Someone had brought Mr. Holmes, always a seeker of novel adventures, to sample outrigger canoeing at the reef. Later, Holmes wrote that "there before me is the Princess

Kaiulani, her face aglow with excitement, shouting and paddling frantically, her eyes flashing with the wild pleasure of it all, as doubtless the eyes of her princely ancestors flashed in the days when surfing was exclusively a royal sport."

He was already contemplating certain possibilities which he mentioned to her when they actually met, a few evenings later, at a party given by Marshal Brown and his wife. Obviously, Mr. Holmes had been "taken up" by his countrymen in Honolulu. He was convinced of the haole version of the overthrow. He wrote of that dinner:

> But let me now present our host and hostess—the gallant Marshal of the Islands, in his uniform of snowy duck, and his charming wife, who raises her glass as if to drink to speedy Annexation. But this toast is not even proposed; courtesy forbids; for in the place of honor at the Marshal's right sits a young girl to whom Annexation means the abandonment of hope, the end of her dreams of royalty.
>
> Princess Kaiulani, niece of the ex-Queen and heiress to the throne of Hawaii, sits there in friendly converse with those who, had it not been for the mistakes of Liliuokalani, would have been compelled to bend the knee to her as subjects. As it is, she is Queen in the hearts of many, although her disappointments and sorrows have tinged her character with just a shade of bitterness, for it is difficult to be resigned to a career so different from that which fortune promised. . . . It is not possible to meet a throneless queen, especially if she be twenty-one years old and pretty, and not become a rabid royalist.

Mr. Holmes mentioned during that evening his hope that she would participate in an intended filming of several Island scenes, which he might build into his principal lecture for the coming season. Intrigued by his animated photographs, Kaiulani agreed. Once it was known that he intended to record "a special series of motion pictures illustrating Hawaiian Life and Customs, and the visit of the United States Manila Expedition to Honolulu," there were no vacant seats at any of the remaining Holmes lectures. Patriotism demanded that this lion (who could spread to America the saga of the Republic's loyalty) be truly lionized.

Thursday, the last day of the month, had been set by Mr. Holmes for photographing the sequence in which Kaiulani was to take part. The *Bulletin* on that same day made announcement of an amendment to the Republic's salaries bill in the House of Representatives, in which the Senate had "concurred without demur." The amendment raised the former meager pension for Kaiulani to a still far from royal six thousand dollars.

At the hour set for the filming, the "cast" recruited by Mr. Holmes assembled at the beach. The scene was to be of surfing in canoes, and six boatloads were participating. In addition to Kaiulani herself, the Browns and Eva Parker and others equally well known in Honolulu life made up what was referred to as the "embarkation." For hours, while Mr. De Pue handled his special cameras to get full advantage of the light, they rode beachward on one spectacular wave after another.

Between "takes," the surfers were given interesting glimpses into the techniques by which they would be made to move as if alive before next winter's American lecture audiences. The pictures used were made at the rate of eighteen to the second, the effect of motion being achieved by displaying them in rapid succession. The impressions, or "negatives," made during the afternoon, said the photographer, would be prepared and colored in the States from projection on a screen. If ever "motion pictures" progressed from their present status as a novelty to become that mass-entertainment medium some dreamers predicted, it would be amusing to be counted among their very earliest performers!

Oppressive heat settled over the city. In early summer came a vigorous American writer named Mabel Craft, to study the Islands for independent reports to important American newspapers. A woman without bias, she investigated the Republic of Hawaii and came to deplore it.

"I do not believe that might necessarily makes right," she maintained in print, for readers in a country now considering the annexation of Hawaii. "And . . . the looting of the Hawaiian monarchy by a few Americans was a sort of successful Jameson Raid, and not an exploit over which any American need thrill with pride."

The Fourth of July, this year of 1898, was celebrated almost with frenzy. Kaiulani watched with silent contempt as officials of a supposedly sovereign government now turned themselves inside out to prove that they were loyal Americans. The Hawaiians remained off the streets, leaving the flags and fireworks to the usurpers.

Continuing to do her duty as she saw it, Kaiulani served as patroness for a performance given at the Opera House on July 6 in honor of American soldiers and officers then in port. The attraction was Dante, billed as the "Greatest Living Magician." His celebrated illusions, including the Japanese Trunk Mystery and the Beggar's Dream, did indeed astonish the house—mostly in American uniform—into agreement with the advance announcement that "Dante approaches nearer the supernatural than any magician living or dead."

The papers of the eleventh quietly announced that "the case of the Dowager Queen Kapiolani vs. Prince David and Cupid . . . has been amicably settled." Kaiulani rejoiced that the rift between her aunt and her cousins had been mended without more bitterness, for at this particular time when any day might see their homeland taken over by a foreign power it was especially important to spare the natives any quarrel among their alii.

On July 13, the blow all supporters of Hawaiian independence had feared for so long finally fell. The loss of their nation became a known fact.

On that morning, the S.S. *Coptic* was sighted off Diamond Head, harbor bound and with a message spelled out by her signal flags. Hawaii had been annexed as part of the United States of America! The news was instantly telephoned to the Executive Building, to Minister Harold Sewall, to American Consul Hayward. Screaming whistles informed the rest of the city. The crowd poured down to the waterfront to greet the ship bringing tidings long awaited or long dreaded.

Mr. Sewall was wreathed in smiles as hundreds of fellow haoles pumped his hand. Fireworks long in readiness began to detonate all through the streets. Guns on the lawn of the erstwhile palace boomed their greeting. Soon, headlines were trumpeting victoriously: ANNEXATION! HERE TO STAY! AND THE STAR SPANGLED BANNER IN TRIUMPH SHALL WAVE O'ER THE ISLES OF HAWAII AND THE HOMES OF THE BRAVE!

The *Coptic* had brought with it a special gift to President Dole (now, of course, former President, as the Republic ceased to exist) from the United States Secretary of State. This was an unofficial American flag upon which forty-six stars were displayed instead of the orthodox forty-five, the extra one signifying Hawaii.

Among the whirlwind rumors flying about the city, those next few days, one claimed that Kaiulani would soon leave Hawaii forever and make her permanent home in England. This tale became so widespread that Papa issued an official denial to the *Commercial Advertiser*. "Her interests are all here," he stated. "She has a deep love for the land of her birth, and a sincere affection for her people."

The published statement went on to give particulars: "For several months past the Princess has been in very poor health and feels the need of a change of climate. For this reason she will go to the country place of Mr. Samuel Parker, in Mana, Hawaii, early in August for a stay of perhaps two months. . . . She has delayed her departure for Mana to await the arrival of her aunt, ex-Queen Liliuokalani, whom she has seen but once—and that for a few hours only—in nearly ten years."

Aunt Liliu was really coming home! The family at Ainahau knew it long before the public was told. She was already on her way westward, accompanied by loyal Heleluhe and his wife, and was to sail for Hawaii aboard the *Gaelic* after a brief stay in San Francisco.

21: Old Glory

The *Gaelic* was sighted off Koko Head, the night of August 1, on what Mable Craft later described as "a perfect midnight. The sky was a deep purple, set with stars and curtained with clouds. At intervals the light of the full moon spilled over the rim of the cloud bank and showed the city crowded between green water and green hills."

Every road into town came alive at the news with hundreds of dark figures all moving in the same direction, like leaves on a stream. Gathering along the waterfront, utterly quiet, the watchers stared across the harbor with set faces—Hawaiian faces, most of them. The haoles were a mere sprinkling. Kaiulani, driven hastily in from Waikiki, sat in her carriage on the wharf. Across intervening heads she saw Koa, accompanied by a band of steadfast royalists, down at the water's very edge.

One by one, like water lilies unfolded, the harbor buoys reflected the ship's own lights to guide the *Gaelic* past sunken coral fangs. Now the incoming vessel loomed in full view against a dimly shining horizon. The pilot boat put off into the darkness. Hawaiian women clung to one another and wept. Liliuokalani had returned from other stubborn struggles in her nation's behalf, but tonight all hope was gone. Her only remaining throne was in their hearts. Miss Craft, somewhere in the crowd, would write, "Adversity has compensations. . . . Had Liliuokalani

177

remained a Queen, she would never have known how much her people loved her."

The *Gaelic*'s bulk drifted closer and slid up alongside the crowded pier. A little canvas enclosure had been erected to protect Auntie from prying eyes and from her carriage Kaiulani watched Koa and his companions quickly mount to the deck and disappear within the tent. A few minutes later Auntie could be seen crossing the open deck with a hand on Koa's sleeve, but moving too erectly to need his assistance. She wore black from head to toe, her face composed and sad under the nodding plumes of her hat. At the gangplank's head she paused for an instant, looking down. A solid mass of upturned faces met that compassionate, tender glance. But the graveyard silence remained unbroken. There were no cheers.

"Aloha!" she said, at last, across the rapt stillness. Her voice rang as rich and strong as ever, despite its softness. "Aloha!"

Their answers roared up as one answer: *"Aloha!"*

When she started down the gangplank, the crowd surged forward as if to touch her as she passed. But no hand actually reached out. They were weeping, men and women alike, and not ashamed of it. They made way as Auntie crossed the pier on Koa's arm, followed closely by her small entourage. As the black plumes drew closer, Kaiulani stepped down in greeting. For a moment, tired dark eyes looked directly into hers. Then she stretched out her arms.

Their public greeting was necessarily brief. Another moment and Koa had handed both of them up into the carriage and was settling himself beside them. Now, belatedly, the scattering of Englishmen and Americans in the crowd bethought themselves to offer three hearty cheers. Auntie bowed a grave acknowledgment as these rang out, for they were intended as a kindness. But her true welcome, Kaiulani knew, had been Hawaiian silence and Hawaiian tears.

Once they had driven away from the pier, the familiar streets of downtown Honolulu lay deserted and dark under the sailing moon. The party in the carriage rode almost silently. This was no moment for trivial conversation. Still in silence, the carriage swerved at last from Beretania Street into the brief driveway leading to Washington Place. The big square white house, girt with its balconies and its forests of foliage, had been waiting like the rest of the one-time kingdom.

Two chamberlains stood by the entrance gates, and two more near the main doors, each holding aloft a blazing kukui torch. Flickering light illuminated the gardens. The torch bearers were old native men, long attached to the Queen's household. They would stand as they were, as if rooted, until morning.

The passengers were helped down from the carriage. They moved up the steps and through a garlanded doorway, only half aware of dim figures of Hawaiians scattered through the grounds. Devoted maids took charge of the returned traveler, while Kaiulani and Koa withdrew, still silently, into the morning room to wait.

Changed into a gown of black and lavender, with diamonds like newly shed tears flashing on her strong hands, the Queen reappeared at last and was seated in her dining room at a plain deal table no more ornate than many a kitchen table in America. Yet she sat at it alone, for no one in the land might sit unbidden in the presence of Majesty. Adoring attendants waved white kahilis over her in a slow rhythm as she ate.

When her meal was cleared away, the line of those who had waited patiently in the gardens began to form. As each old Hawaiian reached the door, he fell on his knees. Crawling thus, he passed before his Queen. Most of the folk in that crawling line were white-haired. One of them, so ancient that his face was wizened like a monkey's, was totally blind. Yet he needed no cane to guide him with the others, or to find the royal hand when his turn came to kiss it.

Aunt Liliu knew each of them of old, called each bent figure by name, eyed each bowed head with tenderness. Outside, the ancient chanters—the *olioli* singers—kept up a witchlike lament. The aged torch bearers still stood statue-still, lifting their flaming brands.

Dawn was pink before Kaiulani's carriage rolled homeward. Tonight, she had stood watch beside Hawaii's own bier. A new

Hawaii might be waiting to be born. But none of those old ones she was leaving behind could realize that. All that they loved was finished, gone forever.

"*Ua ohi pakahi ia aku nei e ka po,*" she murmured, to the clip-clop of the horses. It was an old Hawaiian phrase, recollected from she knew not where. "The night has taken them, one by one."

Not surprisingly, the haole version of Auntie's homecoming attempted belittlement. Tuesday's papers spoke of her only as "Mrs. Dominis." But at Washington Place she was the Queen. On the day after her arrival the old custom of *hookupu,* or gift-bearing, was revived in her honor. Natives thronged to the Dominis mansion carrying their offerings. Even the poorest could present poi wrapped in ti leaves; the richer offered live chickens with bound legs or trussed and squealing pigs. There was no attempt at rivalry here, only the aloha in their hearts which prompted them to give cheerfully, even though afterward they might go hungry.

Not one of the hundreds flooding her gardens had come seeking any favor or advantage for himself. Preferments were no longer the Queen's to bestow. Yet, from ragged beggars to alii, they came. Honolulu's business was left for the day to its paler-skinned overlords. The haoles made no mention whatever of this touching event in their newspapers, which so often talked of "native disgust with the monarchy."

For the most part, during the first days of August, Kaiulani remained at home in her garden. In the city, the same days stretched out hot and sunny and charged with the excitement of what was to come. The tiny capital of the Kamehamehas was buzzing with more rumors than ever. It was said that Admiral Miller, in charge of the annexation ceremonies, was decently sensitive to the grief of the Hawaiians and was planning a simple ritual rather than a Roman holiday.

Only the riffraff, Papa reported, were making a carnival of the event now so close upon them. A few people flaunted tawdry badges depicting Uncle Sam embracing a dusky female, Miss Hawaii, more African than Polynesian, over the motto "This Is Our Wedding Day." But these men were not the prominent annexationists. One carriage rolled about the streets decked out in red-white-and-blue bunting; but it belonged to a wealthy Greek merchant, not to an American. In Papa's judgment—for he was a just man, even in final defeat—the leaders who had fought hardest for annexation now did little gloating over their victory.

"Many a man who worked years to overthrow the monarchy," he said, "now has a mist in his eyes when he passes the Palace where the old flag will be hauled down." It seemed a bit too late for haole tears!

Kaiulani was waited upon by a naval messenger with her official invitation to attend the ceremonies of annexation, at noon on the twelfth of August. She thanked Admiral Miller's representative and sent her regrets. And she declined another invitation: at the nearby American Legation, on the afternoon of Annexation Day, the Sewalls' infant son Arthur was to be christened. Though she appreciated the kind intention of their request that she be present, Kaiulani felt strongly that she should make no public appearance on the day of her people's deepest sorrow. A friendly refusal was sent to the Legation. Ainahau drew in upon itself and waited.

As the afternoon of August 11 faded into evening, a strange heaviness slowed the breeze. The palms were still. The distant mountains seemed empty humps against the stars. But any true Hawaiian, on this night of waiting, knew that the mountains were not empty.

Back in the hills, high in the valleys, the old kahunas were muttering their supplications, asking the gods for a downpour to drench the new flags waiting to be raised in the morning. It seemed as though their prayers were to be answered. All through the late night, rain hit like fists against Honolulu windows. It was still falling at dawn.

But by ten o'clock, the torrent had thinned. Ten was the hour set for the Hawaiian National Guard to form at its barracks and begin a march to the waterfront. They were to escort the crew of the U.S.S. *Philadelphia* from the docks to the palace for the ceremonies.

Ainahau seemed quite empty. Under her banyan, Kaiulani sat listening to the stillness. No single shout lifted, this morning, from the surf at Waikiki. The peacocks sulked and avoided the wet grass.

Eleven o'clock. The crowd at Papa Moi's once-proud palace would be moving past the gates in force now, the rich in their carriages, the poor on foot. On lawns still gleaming from rain, they would be finding places; Chinese, placid and almond-eyed; Japanese women in their butterfly kimonos; Portuguese wearing the gaudy kerchiefs they had brought with them from the Azores; Americans, of course; but few Hawaiians in the throng—very few Hawaiians.

For Hawaiians, this was a day of execution. The windows of every native residence, from Washington Place to the humblest hut, would be shuttered. Though the kanakas loved music and parades, this one celebration—the most significant in all Hawaii's history—would be observed without them.

Eleven-thirty. The Government Band must be marching past the gates now, colors flying. Hawaiian colors still. Hawaiian flags until the stroke of noon. Bluejackets from the *Philadelphia* would march behind the music, and then an honor guard bearing the American banner. Ladies in the stands must be fanning themselves daintily against the muggy heat. How many among them would have wound *ilima* around their hats, as in former days, the golden leis of royalty now deposed?

Eleven-forty-five. Time for the crowd to rise respectfully as their ex-President and his Cabinet took their places—Mr. Dole looking elegant and grave, like a man at a very fashionable party where no one was having fun. Time for Minister Sewall and Admiral Miller to appear.

Time for the bared heads of all those present to bow in a last solemn prayer for God's mercies upon all the sons and daughters of Hawaii. And then for the brief interchange of formal phrases by which Minister Sewall would officially accept the sovereignty offered to his government.

A few brief minutes until noon . . .

The band would be playing its beloved "Hawaii Ponoi" for a last time as a free nation's anthem; old Captain Berger, who had composed the air so long ago to fit Kalakaua's words, leading them with tears in his eyes. The troops would present arms. And from the waterfront . . .

No need only to imagine that deep booming of the *Philadelphia*'s guns, or the answer of the shore battery, even so far away as Ainahau. The Hawaiian flag was lowering. And Hawaiians were Americans now.

22: In the Afterglow

Hawaii's separate sun was set forever. But now, in its afterglow, there still was hope for a despoiled people. Under American control, they no longer could be deprived of the vote. It now lay within their power, as it had not since the overthrow, to fight for their rights with democracy's weapons. The unbroken old woman who had been their Queen meant to see that they were exploited no longer—and Kaiulani found, during the rest of that annexation summer, that she was at Washington Place helping Auntie almost as much as she was at Ainahau.

President McKinley's commissioners had arrived in Honolulu soon after the annexation ceremonies, and the Hawaiian Patriotic League at once urged them to grant full American citizenship to all native citizens, "that we may not become aliens and pariahs in our own country, to be treated like a conquered people." The commissioners, together with ex-President Dole and Judge Walter Frear, representing Hawaii, would presently draw up recommendations for an Organic Act to establish a future government for the new Territory of Hawaii.

Senators John T. Morgan of Alabama and Shelby Collum of Kentucky, Congressman Robert Hitt of Illinois, and others of their visiting party, were being beseiged by every special interest in the Islands. The voices of the Hawaiians themselves must not be drowned out. To this task both Liliuokalani and Kaiulani now dedicated themselves.

Mabel Craft, who lingered in the Islands to complete her story of this momentous summer, drew a perceptive comparison between the old woman and the young:

> Liliuokalani has money, and keeps quite a retinue . . . at Washington Place. This house is her private residence, coming to her from her husband. It is a big fine building, in the old Southern plantation style, with a veranda all around and pillars that suggest the White House. . . .
>
> Ordinarily the Queen dines alone, fanned by white *kahilis* wielded by pretty native girls. Her tastes are simple and have not been changed by travel or years of exile. She is still an ardent lover of *poi* and of fish *au naturel,* and . . . is the only person I have seen who can eat a mango gracefully. The Queen still wears the national *holoku* with extreme grace. . . . She is exceedingly gracious to Americans, but with her former subjects she maintains that reserve which is a royal prerogative.
>
> The menage of Princess Kaiulani at Ainahau (cool place), on the road to Waikiki, is much more Americanized. She clings outwardly to Hawaiian customs, and seldom appears without a royal *lei* of *oo* feathers, but her household is Caucasian. . . . Her drawingroom is entirely modern, with its photographs and fauteuils, and might be in Belgravia or Fifth Avenue. The feather *kahilis* that adorn the corners are the only reminders of barbaric royalty. . . . This refined and gently bred girl is a model of the feminine graces and proprieties. Only a royal temper and a will of her own that brooks no contradiction have descended to this daughter of fiery chiefs. It is a far cry from Kalakaua . . . to this delicately sublimated niece of his.

The commissioners were planning a tour of inspection of the Big Island, and Auntie intended to make the same journey— confident that the commission could not fail to be influenced by the spectacle of her former subjects' loyalty. Kaiulani and Koa accompanied her to her inter-island steamer on the morning of August 21. Erect and dignified in her black traveling costume, Auntie was visible on deck until the *Kinau* was well out in the channel.

Reports of the royal excursion trickled back to Ainahau. Auntie opened her campaign to impress the commissioners when the *Kinau* dropped anchor off Kailua. The Hawaiians had opened the stately "House of Kings" there to receive their distinguished visitors. A mass meeting had been arranged and a luau was awaiting them.

But Auntie, made wise by bitter experience in the arts of surprise attack, let it be known ashore that she was indisposed and felt unequal to landing. Instantly, the crowd deserted the reception and poured down to the waterfront. Since their Queen would not come ashore to her luau, the luau was loaded into canoes and paddled out to the *Kinau*. Swarming up the ship's side, the bearers of the feast passed before Her Majesty on their knees to present what they had brought. Let the startled commissioners ashore observe, and judge how the natives greeted annexation!

Similar strategy met similar success after the landing at Hilo. The commissioners had scheduled a trip to the volcano. The Queen (by seeming coincidence) announced a similar junket of her own. Both parties were large, accommodations at the crater woefully few. The Americans were simply left to fend for themselves. All available space at once was turned over to the Queen. In the public rooms at the summit shelter the two groups met socially, and Auntie was never more the cultured *grande dame*. The commissioners were reported as deeply impressed, to a man.

At home, awaiting news of this pilgrimage, Kaiulani merely marked time. Auntie returned to Oahu aboard the *Kinau* on August 29. So did the American commissioners. And now Honolulu really flung itself into entertaining the all-important visitors. On September 1, Mrs. W. C. Wilder gave an elaborate reception to the commission's ladies at Eskbank, the beautiful Wilder home, and Kaiulani appeared at the party, smiling unfailingly, doing her best to support Auntie's campaign to win the regard of these haoles for the Hawaiians.

Next day, Aunt Liliu celebrated her sixtieth birthday at Washington Place with a reception at high noon. For two hours an unbroken line of callers filed past the erect figure to pay homage. The *Hui Leahi*—that organization of the gallant veterans of the Diamond Head battle of January 1895, who under the Republic had kept its existence a secret but who now feared no reprisals—marched through the streets in a body to attend, led by the National Band. Commissioners might observe these honors being paid to the ex-Queen and draw their own conclusions.

Kaiulani's own contribution to the education of the commission was made a few days later, on September 7. She opened Ainahau for a luau which even the opposition press had to admit was "brilliant" in its design to "show the strangers the true Hawaiian manner of feasting." Auntie came out from town to grace the entertainment.

Wearing a brocaded satin holoku of royal yellow, a golden lei of *oo* feathers crowning her dark hair, Kaiulani presented a carefully calculated picture of Polynesian charm as she received her guests. A military band stationed under the banyan entertained with "Sweet Adeline," "A Hot Time in the Old Town Tonight," and others of the latest airs. The usual before-dinner stiffness melted rapidly. Japanese lanterns bloomed like flowers of light from every shrub and tree.

When the time for feasting arrived, Kaiulani took Senator Collum's arm. Three tables set with forty places apiece occupied the large lanai, each decked with green ferns, scarlet crab apples, golden oranges, and pink watermelon. Two by two, the guests of honor and then the remainder of the gathering followed her.

The girls and young matrons of Kaiulani's own circle—Helen Parker, Kate Vida, Rosie Robertson—all wore holokus, and not by accident. As the leis of pink carnation or green maile woven for each guest were donned, the tables took on a more and more Polynesian air.

Holoku-clad servants were stationed behind Kaiulani's own place and Auntie's—and behind that of Koa, handsome and urbane at one of the side tables—waving kahilis to complete the picture of royalty dining as it had of yore. Kaiulani put a finishing touch to the portrait by dipping a dainty finger into the calabash of pasty poi before her.

Across the table, she observed Mrs. Collum eying the array of native dishes with mild alarm and finally making her selection with a murmured "One is always *sure* of chicken." But Mrs. Hitt, completely in the spirit of the occasion, took to poi with a jaunty disregard for forks or spoons. Senator Collum plunged into the feast with an abandoned disregard for tomorrow, while Senator Morgan attacked the watermelon.

Only when the diners were sighing for mercy was the feast ended. Guests strolled along the lantern-lit paths and waited for the lanai to be cleared for dancing. Ainahau had not witnessed such prolonged gaiety for many a year.

While Kaiulani and Aunt Liliu were carrying on this campaign to convince the commission of the civilization and the devotion of the Hawaiians, others who had fared badly at the hands of haole usurpers were fighting the same native battle more directly. The Hawaiian National League drew up an appeal to be presented to the commissioners. This document contained four specific pleas: that Hawaii be made a Territory of the United States; that the Hawaiian flag be retained as flag of this Territory; that pensions be granted the ladies of the deposed Royal Family, Queen Liliuokalani, Princess Kaiulani, and Dowager Queen Kapiolani; and, most important of all, that male suffrage be made universal, with only an educational qualification for voters.

The late Republic's leaders had anticipated no difficulty in perpetuating their former voting rules. Now, faced with a robbed people's determination to the contrary, they began moving heaven and earth to sway Congressional opinion in their favor. Word came from Washington that the weapon of ridicule was being wielded mercilessly there. A scurrilous burlesque called *The Hula Girl* was mocking the Hawaiian cause. Its cast included "Queen Lil"; a "Princess Koylani"; a character, "Jole," who satirized the ex-Republic's president; and a fat, gross comedian irreverently tagged "Rover Greveland."

Speculation seethed as to who would become the Territory's first governor. The powers of the defunct Republic began quarreling among themselves. Mr. Dole was one possibility. But Dr. J. S. McGrew, ardent propagandist for the haoles and known as the "father of annexation," advanced his own candidacy. The *Advertiser's* man, understandably, was its own Lorrin Thurston.

The *Bulletin*'s editor advocated Minister Sewall. Both the fiery Robert Wilcox and the Big Island rancher Samuel Parker tossed their hats into the ring. The *Independent* championed Aunt Liliu, hopeful that she might rule again even without scepter.

Kaiulani was suggested for the governorship in certain quarters, and Mama's one-time service in a similar post was recalled to support the proposal. But even Kaiulani's stanchest advocates did not (in view of her youth and sex) take their cause too seriously.

In mid-September, with Eva and Helen Parker, she departed for a week's rest up Manoa Valley at the home of her half-sister Helen Boyd. In the quiet green valley, those shrill voices back in Honolulu arguing the governorship seemed faint and very far away.

Her "week" with the Boyds stretched to a longer absence, and it was October 12 before Kaiulani was home again at Ainahau. The month wore itself out in trivial occupations. On October 19, she and Papa gave a reception for two hundred guests. On the night of October 25, they again were hosts for a dancing party which earned the *Advertiser*'s prediction, "an enjoyable time is expected, as the Princess always succeeds in doing her part at any of her home gatherings." On Tuesday, the last day of the month, she held her final "at home" for the season.

November began with a reception in honor of the Mikado's birthday, given by Japan's Consul, Miki Saito. It was the last important social event before Auntie again left the Islands for an indefinite stay in Washington—there to urge political recognition for her Hawaiians, and to press her claim for indemnity for the confiscation of her Crown Lands and her throne.

As always on the departure of one of their alii, the natives were at the wharf in force to watch the *Coptic* weigh anchor. Auntie sat at the railing of the upper deck to give them a good view of her, laden with *leis*. Surrounding her, until a belated "All ashore" was sounded, were Kaiulani and Papa and Koa and a handful of others.

Colonel Macfarlane, for so many years Auntie's confidential advisor, was also in the party. He was to write of it, later:

> The boat was delayed, and although the hour was late and Kaiulani delicate she refused to leave, and stayed on board some five hours to see the last of her aunt. Any heart must have been touched at the sight of those two royal women clinging together in their fallen dignity. I was trying to console Kaiulani with some cheerful prospects.
>
> "All has not been taken from you," I said. "The American Government respects your position and will help you to keep it up. Your aunt will receive an income that will still enable her to live as an ex-Queen. You will still be able to live as an ex-Princess; your birth and your antecedents will never be forgotten, and you will remain a leader of society here, the first lady in the land."
>
> "Yes," she answered me, with a tired smile, "but I shan't be much of a real Princess, shall I? They haven't left me much to live for." And as she spoke she caught her hand to her side, and I could see the rapid beating of her heart.
>
> "I don't talk about it," she went on; "I try not to grieve my father, who watches over me so devotedly and seeks to make up to me with his love for all I have lost. For his sake, I try not to mind, to appear bright and happy. But I think my heart is broken."
>
> Then she remembered herself as a Princess. "There is one last thing I would like to say," she added. "Whatever my aunt attempts to do, whatever she wishes or approves, I am with her. All Liliuokalani's decisions will have my adhesion and signature."

Almost immediately upon arriving back in the American capital, the Queen sent her niece some charming pictures of Washington. Thanking her from Ainahau, Kaiulani permitted herself a rare expression of bitterness:

> Daily we as a great race are being subjected to a great deal of misery and the more I see of the American soldiers about town the more I am unable to tolerate them, what they stand for and the way we are belittled it is enough to ruin one's faith in God.
>
> Last week some Americans came to the house and knocked rather violently at the door, and when they had stated their cause, they wished to know if it would be permissable for the EX-Princess

to have her picture taken with them. Oh, will they never leave us alone? They have now taken away everything from us and it seems there is left but little, and that little our very life itself. . . .

We live now in such a semi-retired way . . . that people wonder if we even exist any more. I too wonder, and to what purpose?

On the first of December, Andrew Adams reappeared in town from the sugar fields at Ewa, where he had gone as an overseer after quitting his job on the newspaper. He was on holiday before taking up new work at the Spreckelsville plantation. Andrew was as attentive as ever, and frequently at Ainahau. It was impossible not to read in Papa's eyes a lingering thought that the romance he had approved at last might be developing.

But nothing was further from Kaiulani's own intention. She did not permit Andrew's arrival to change her plans for going to the Big Island on December 7. The steamer *Kinau* took her and her maid aboard, along with other gay guests—all bound for the giant house party which was to celebrate Eva Parker's wedding at Mana, the Parker family's storied ranch.

23: The Spear of Waimea

The Parker ranch had been a Hawaiian legend for three-quarters of a century. On high acres first cleared in Kamehameha I's time by the original haole John Palmer Parker and his Hawaiian wife Kipikane, the earliest Mana house had been built all of koa wood sawed on the place, even to the wooden nails pinning it together. As the Parker herds of cattle grew, outbuildings clustered around the original house—a dairy, a meat house, cisterns, servants' quarters, a saddle room, sheds for the plows and the bullock wagons.

In later times, John's two sons—John II and Eben—had lived with their own Hawaiian wives like royalty on the vast acreage, and after them, Eben's son Sam, the present owner—the dashing "Cowboy of Waimea." By Sam's day, Parker herds by the thousands grazed the plains between Waimea and Mana, and the ranch was like a private empire.

Sam Parker had married one of the great Hawaiian beauties, Panana Napela, whose father was descended from the Kings of Maui. Both fond of entertaining, they had enlarged Mana and developed its beautiful gardens. Their daughters Eva and Helen had been brought up like princesses, much as had Kaiulani herself. On December 14, Eva was to marry her first cousin, Frank Woods.

Christmas was a royal feast at Mana, yet no more than an epilogue to the wedding for which the guests had gathered. In the

gay round of events, no one really took time to notice when the
year of annexation faded into 1899. All the old Big Island families were contributing their separate entertainments to the busy
days.

Guests housed at Mana proper made frequent expeditions to
other Parker homes—to the one called Waiemi, a stopping-off
point on the trail from Mana to Kawaihae on the coast, or perhaps to another house at Kawaihae itself, especially popular in
the *aku* and *akule* fishing seasons.

Here Sam Parker kept his ordinary canoes and double fishing
canoes in boathouses on the beach. This Kawaihae house was
fascinating, too, in that its two bedrooms were said to be haunted
and no one would sleep in them. Only the front lanai and the
kitchen were used, and when a gay party stayed there overnight,
its members slept on mats in the open under mosquito netting
strung from the trees.

It was here that guests were put ashore off the inter-island
steamer from Honolulu. The Parkers scorned to use local wharves,
but sent out canoes manned by sturdy Hawaiian crews to ferry
in new arrivals to their own wide beach.

But Mana, high on the mountain, was the heart of the empire.
The main house and its out-buildings had never really lost their
rugged ranch character. Yet inside the sturdy walls, luxury
bloomed. Panana Parker's wedding silver, lovingly tended by
native servants, gleamed proudly throughout the spacious rooms.
It was the custom here to dress for dinner, with the ladies all
wearing flowers.

Good-looking Sam Woods, another Parker cousin and like
herself over from Honolulu for the wedding festivities, was Kaiulani's usual escort at these holiday amusements. Although somewhat younger than she, Sam was so attentive that rumors of a
romance began to drift around the Island. Oblivious to them,
Kaiulani continued her efforts to enjoy herself—and to forget
what could not be changed.

In country overrun with game, hunting entertained the sporting bloods among the company. Some adventuresome guests took
lessons in calf roping; for the *paniolos*, with flower leis circling

their broad-brimmed hats, were always ready to herd a few cattle onto a nearby flat plain to provide action for friends of "Mr. Sam." With the swimming parties and picnics, the luaus and dances, and the great central event of Eva's wedding, the time passed swiftly. By January 8, guests were departing. But Kaiulani and a few others stayed on, postponing their return to Honolulu. There was no reason to hurry back to days of artificial cheerfulness.

One guest who shared that Mana visit later wrote of Kaiulani, "No photograph could indicate her graceful winsomeness. Though she could not afford to dress as became her rank, she always looked exquisitely dressed. People used to say that if she got hold of a few yards of material and wound them about her she would contrive to look fashionably attired."

The day in mid-January when a group of the Parkers' lingering guests started on a picnic ride from the high ranch began with fair weather. But when the riders were well out on the mountain trail, the sharp-driven Waimea rain began to assault them. This famous "horizontal rain" of the region might set in at any hour, damp and cold, so pitiless that an old proverb said, "Waimea is like a spear rubbed by the wind, as the cold spray is blown by the *kipuupuu* rain."

At Mana, raincoats were always carried rolled on saddles, and Kaiulani's companions called to her to put hers on. But while she was laughing at their sensible advice, recklessness prompting her to ignore the shower, she recognized with a certain dismay a bent figure afoot on the trail ahead. He was someone she had no desire to be detained by, and recklessness abruptly became purpose.

This old man had been a Polynesian priest of the old religion —or so people at Mana, explaining him, had told her. As such, he was deeply versed in the pedigrees of the alii which formed so substantial a part of the old rites and chants. His insistence upon the ancient forms, on prostrating himself at the feet of royalty, was as out of key with the modern world as were his drawn-out, droning chronicles of times long gone.

So, as she spied his white head in the rain, Kaiulani straightened in her saddle. "Let's gallop ahead before he can stop us!"

And her horse was in the lead as the party flicked their mounts and raced up the trail. She was thoroughly drenched before the thought of an unworn raincoat again occurred to her. By then, the party was on its way back to Mana and she did not take her soaking seriously.

Not until January 24 did Honolulu papers print the postscript to that forgetfulness: "Princess Kaiulani is quite ill at the Parker home at Mana, Hawaii. Governor Cleghorn leaves for Mana on the *'Kinau'* today."

Papa brought with him their devoted family physician, Doctor Walters, and within two weeks Honolulu readers could be told that "Princess Kaiulani is much improved in health. . . . She and her father Gov. A. S. Cleghorn will return from Mana by the next *'Kinau.'*

With this assurance, the city could assume that her illness was not serious. A petition to President McKinley and his Congress was circulated, urging an official pension for her. The *Advertiser*'s lead editorial of February 5 praised the undertaking. As one writer later said:

> Everyone admired her attitude. They could not do otherwise. Her dignity, her pathetic resignation, her silent sorrow appealed to all. The natives loved her for her quiet, steadfast sympathy with their woe, her uncomplaining endurance of her own; the whites admired her for her stately reserve, her queenly display of all necessary courtesy while holding herself aloof from undue intimacy. It was impossible not to love her.

On February 9, the *Kinau* having sailed without her and the *Mauna Loa* being scheduled to depart, Kaiulani was carried on a litter from the mountain ranch to Kawaihae and then out to the waiting steamer. Doctor Walters had diagnosed her symptoms as those of inflammatory rheumatism, but later he said they were complicated by exophthalmic goiter. By the morning of the sailing, the pain had diminished except in the left side of her head and in her left forearm.

Actually, once she was safely back at Ainahau, the family were more concerned about Kuhio than about her. He came home on February 11 from a vacation with his wife on Kauai. And the sumptuous Princess Elizabeth's account of how Kuhio's horse had stumbled—throwing him into line with its hoofs and also into the trap of a rock crevice—was sufficiently dramatic to overshadow the mere lingering after-effects of a "cold."

On February 17 the papers ran the full text of the petition in Kaiulani's favor being made ready for submission to Washington; and with it, personal comment which read like a belated valentine. The editors explained that the petition might have received many thousand signatures in the Territory, but that a decision had been made by its sponsors to limit the signing to men actively participating in the overthrow. Their names would be tacit proof that no objection could be found.

Said the *Advertiser:*

> The quiet efforts of Princess Kaiulani to obliterate the harsh feelings growing out of the change of government in Hawaii, and her acceptance of the new order of things, is appreciated by this community. And by none more so than those who were directly instrumental in bringing that change about. . . . Whether the object of the petition is successful or not, it is a strong tribute by active political opponents to the character and worth of Kaiulani."

Sitting beside her bed, Papa read her the news stories. For some reason her illness still refused to yield to treatment as Doctor Walters had expected; and a few days later, disturbed by its continuance, he summoned in a colleague for consultation. Helen Cleghorn Boyd, who through the years had taken over so many of Mama's duties, moved out to Waikiki to take charge of the household. Friends from the city called daily, concerned but not yet alarmed.

Papa seldom left the sickroom. But the rest of the family were so little worried that Kuhio and Elizabeth did not hesitate to leave on February 23 for Kona—Kuhio by now being sufficiently recovered from his misadventure.

At the beginning of March her doctors knew that their patient's illness had taken a turn for the worse, and that rheumatism was again invading the region of her heart. Still, there were good prospects of controlling it. Kaiulani, lying in her darkened room, could rouse herself sufficiently to express regret at missing the bazaar and *luau* being given by a favorite charity, the Hawaiian Relief Society.

Early on Sunday evening, the fifth of March, 1899, the doctors issued one of their frequent bulletins to the press. It stated: "The Princess rested better on Saturday night. She was able to get a little sleep. She had a bad turn Sunday morning, but as the day progressed there was an improvement. . . . Altogether, it can be said that the young lady is slightly better, but not yet entirely out of danger."

But just after midnight more alarming word came from the sickroom where both doctors labored. Frightened servants scattered to assemble the family.

By half-past one, Papa was in the room where she lay breathing unsteadily, eyes half-closed. Her half-sisters, Helen and Rosie, and Kate Vida and Helen Parker had come; and Koa too, although Papa had not fully approved of the Prince's being summoned. There seemed to be other presences stirring in the shadows of the room.

The creeping hands of the clocks had reached precisely the hour of two when Kaiulani stirred on her bed and cried out a single frightened word—so blurred that afterward some who heard it claimed it was "Mama!" and others that it had been "Koa!"

And then, as that morning's *Advertiser* said: "The silver thread by which life had been hanging snapped like the overtaxed string of a fine stringed instrument. And there passed away she who was the most beloved of all the Hawaiian race."

Oahu did not have to wait for its morning newspapers to bring news of the tragedy. Almost immediately, and even at a distance halfway to town from Ainahau, people were startled from their sleep by a sudden wild screaming in the night. Kaiulani's peacocks were crying out their loss as if they consciously comprehended it.

Later it was realized that the sudden comings and goings at the big house, the unaccustomed lights, must have disturbed the proud birds. But at the time, they seemed to understand. "And we heard them miles away," one friend was to recall, half a century afterward, "and we knew that the Princess had died."

24: A Last Aloha

Even outlying districts were not long in receiving the grievous news. Tuesday's *Advertiser* described the general feeling: "There were many sad hearts and sorrowing homes in Honolulu yesterday. . . . Sad, sad, was the common utterance. . . . In many cases one would think the speaker had lost a member of his or her own family."

From the earliest hours of light on Monday, a stream of carriages passed up and down the driveway at Ainahau. In Honolulu, stunned Hawaiians gathered in fishmarkets and along the waterfront—an unnatural silence the evidence of their grief. Since sun-up, flags on government buildings and foreign consulates had drooped at half-staff.

President Dole convened a morning meeting of his Cabinet, at which it was voted to place at Governor Cleghorn's disposal all official resources in arrangements for a state funeral. But the stricken father had planned that his daughter would lie in state in her own home on Wednesday and afterward would be carried to Kawaiahao Church for a public ceremony. Still dazed by his loss, he requested that the interim government take charge of funeral arrangements. Meanwhile, the steamer *Helene* had already been sent to Hawaii to bring back the dead Princess's relatives and friends there.

Very early on Wednesday morning, Dowager Queen Kapiolani

and her full retinue arrived to take farewell of the girl who lay in a robe of white in the front room of Ainahau, directly off the veranda and faced toward the sea. Raised three feet above the polished floor, the bier was draped in a purple pall embroidered in gold with Kaiulani's own arms. White orchids and orange blossoms were strewn over the dais like tears. To each side of it stood four retainers dressed in somber black, waving above their departed mistress her royal kahilis.

As visitors arrived, ushers guided them through darkened rooms stifling with the perfume of flowers. In the outer parlors sat Hawaiians of the older generation, most of them well able to recall the birth of Kaiulani's mother, Princess Likelike. Under the banyan outside, the Government Band played dirges as the hours passed.

The constant flow of newcomers past the main doors never abated throughout the day. No station nor rank, no race nor color, was unrepresented. President and Mrs. Dole and their official family rubbed shoulders with frock-coated members of the Aloha Aina, and with delegations from the Maternity Home, the Red Cross, the churches.

Representing the family, Jim and Helen Boyd and Rosie Robertson—attended by Koa and Kuhio—acknowledged expressions of sympathy in the public rooms. Archibald Cleghorn remained in his own room.

At six o'clock, after the doors were closed, the house servants of Ainahau were admitted to the front room for a last glimpse of their departed alii. Most of them had been in service with the Cleghorn family since Kaiulani's babyhood. Their devotion to her now broke out in uncontrolled sobs.

At midnight on Friday Kaiulani's body was moved privately to the city. In the early hours of darkness, loyal natives began to gather in Ainahau's gardens, lighting the shadows with torches. The mansion's rigid old master would not quit it until he had stood for one last time beside the girl who had been his reason for building the beautiful house. When he made that last visit to the room where she lay, even the kahili bearers were removed.

For fifteen minutes he remained there alone. Then it was time to go.

As the slow procession made its way along the dark Waikiki road, thousands of Hawaiians appeared out of the night to follow it on foot—their wailing and guttering torches turning back Island history to lost centuries. Two mounted policemen cleared a way for the hearse drawn by sable-draped horses, and behind it followed the official pall-bearers and the petty chiefs and the carriages of the family.

At Kawaiahao, although it was close to two o'clock in the morning, the Bishop of Honolulu and his clergy were waiting, along with several hundred grieving Hawaiians. The white casket was carried inside. Koa and Kuhio were two of those who bore it, Andrew Adams another. A brief, solemn service was conducted by the Bishop over bowed heads.

A group of devoted women had toiled throughout the day to bank the church with flowers and to drape the pillars in white tarlatan wreathed with maile. Above the altar hung the royal standards of Kaiulani and Likelike. The square in which the bier rested was marked off by an arch of white, garlanded in maile.

For the rest of the week the newspapers were filled with references to the Princess's death. One lover of animals commented: "The Princess had at Ainahau a tribe of peafowl and every one of the birds would eat from her hands. . . . The birds have been acting as if they were wondering why she was neglecting them, and so have the horses. Old, faithful Fairy, deserted for a second and last time by his mistress, simply mopes around." An editorial indulged in prophecy: "In the years to come, through all changes of political and social conditions, the story of her life . . . will be told to travelers who come to us from all the seas, and it will make one of the pathetic romances of Hawaii."

At the second lying-in-state, on Saturday, even the heavens wept—as according to tradition they always did upon the death of a high chief. Ignoring the rain, loyal thousands crowded the churchyard. Up the wide steps they poured, to file along the center aisle and pass the white casket. At brief intervals, the old barbaric wailing echoed through the Christian building on a note of broken farewell. One observer wrote:

> At night the scene was intensified in picturesqueness. The light became dimmer, the forms of the watchers grew more indistinct, and everything seemed unreal. . . . The large crowds which had . . . thronged through the day left quite a number who stayed through the night. On the seats were scattered old natives whom weariness had seized and who were fast asleep. . . . The first rays of the rising sun fell upon the little band of watchers as they waved their kahilis to and fro."

By Sunday, the rain was gone. The city was again awash with vivid light. At Kaiulani's own church, St. Andrew's, the empty royal pew was draped in black. At Kawaiahao, the afternoon funeral was to be the day's first service. But by noon the crowds were dense not only in the area around the church but also along streets the procession would travel. Spanking carriages locked wheels with dilapidated buggies. Every hack in the city had been hired. And still the greater mass of thousands kept pouring in afoot, seeking points of vantage.

Many old Hawaiians wore rusty black left over from earlier royal funerals. Others wore mourning holokus, inky black or spotlessly white. Children darted about, in danger from nervous horses. The crowd on the roof of the Opera House grew so dense that police ordered the people down, fearing that the building might collapse.

When at last the doors to Kawaiahao were flung open, a vast wave of humanity surged up the steps seeking admission. The ushers preserved order with admirable fortitude, letting in a certain number and then closing the doors again until these people could be seated.

At one-thirty, the parade began to assemble. The Engineer Corps with gleaming arms and crepe-draped standards marched up and took their places on King Street, followed by the National Guard and the deputations of the various organizations and societies. The polished instruments of the forming bands blazed in the sunlight.

By fifteen minutes before two, when the service was to begin, the pews were packed. During the organ prelude, Governor Cleghorn's party was led up the main aisle to its chairs on the *makai* side of the church, facing the casket. The Justices of the Supreme Court, in flowing robes, were followed into facing positions on the *mauka* side by President and Mrs. Dole, Cabinet members, public officials, military officers.

The service began with the organ *"In Memoriam"* written long ago for the funeral of Princess Likelike. Bishop Willis read the Scriptures. St. Andrew's Choir intoned the Thirty-Ninth Psalm. The native choir of Kawaiahao sang sweetly, in Hawaiian, "Brief Life Is Here Our Portion." Also in Hawaiian, the church's pastor, Rev. H. H. Parker, spoke.

"I want to add my flower to her wreath," he said simply, movingly, "the same as I am sure does every parent and every child in Hawaii *Nei*. Love is a flower transplanted from Heaven, and all who knew Kaiulani loved her. . . . In your lives, follow her example."

The strains of the last song, "Angels Ever Bright and Fair," faded in the church. The white casket was lovingly borne outside to the waiting hearse, and the mourners followed it. Kahilis of fresh green maile intertwined with royal leis of ilima, a last gift from Koa, waved sadly as bugles sounded. Minute guns boomed out across the city. Church bells tolled. The official procession began to move. Two hundred and thirty stalwart native men grasped the black-and-white ropes fixed to the hearse and it began to roll.

In the first of the mourning carriages rode Archibald Cleghorn and his two surviving daughters. The second carriage, empty, represented Liliuokalani, still absent in Washington. In the third were Dowager Queen Kapiolani, Koa, Kuhio, and his Elizabeth. In a fourth, President and Mrs. Dole. The line stretched out.

The streets all along the way were crowded, but beyond the ilima-decked gates to the Royal Mausoleum up Nuuanu Valley only a handful were permitted to follow. The white casket was carried inside to rest before the banks of flowers screening earlier royal crypts. Here the Bishop read the remainder of the Episcopal

Order for the Burial of the Dead. The service ended. The mourners withdrew.

Archibald Cleghorn was the last of them to walk away.

"At last," wrote one sympathetic observer of this moment for his newspaper, "he turned his face toward the door and entering his carriage drove directly to beautiful Ainahau where the sweetest flowers grow, and where the fairest of them all will bloom no more."

Since Then: " Dreaming of Thrones . . ."

No life ends in a funeral. In other lives, in other memories, in influence upon events yet to come, it continues.

Kaiulani's state funeral was not yet a matter of history when whispers concerning her death began to circulate in the city. These won such acceptance that Colonel Macfarlane angrily attacked them:

> "The Princess Kaiulani prayed to death? Nonsense! This kind of exaggerated rumor, based on native tradition, always gets abroad when a royal person dies. Yes, I know the things that were whispered when her mother, Princess Likelike, died. . . . But Kaiulani? Kaiulani was adored by her people. . . . There is not a native in the Islands who could have wished to compass that sweet girl's death. . . ."

Whispers of a gentler sort remembered that the favorite flower of the dead Princess always had been the Chinese jasmine growing in her father's gardens. The blossoms came to be so related in the general mind with her life at Ainahau that they became known in Hawaii as *pikake,* a native phonetic rendition of the word "peacock."

That attempts should be made to convey in verse the nation's overwhelming loss was almost inevitable, and among many poems inspired by Kaiulani's death was one by Philip Henry Dodge:

> Heard ye those winds which sighed and swept
> From sea to sea, while rain-tides wept?

205

Though storms fling on and tempest leaps—
Dark midnight past, the Princess sleeps!

Saw ye that place—the gentle tread,
Kahilis bending, fragrance shed?
Mid all the throng that bows and weeps,
In robes of white the Princess sleeps!

Know ye the crown—no goldsmith arts,
But forged from out a thousand hearts
For her who midst the change of State
Was gracious, triumphing o'er her fate?

For such the world in homage keeps
A crown, although the Princess sleeps.

That peaceful acceptance of American rule into which Kaiulani had led her people by example bore its fruit for them when (on April 30, 1900) an Organic Act set up a government for the new Territory of Hawaii. This document, to be Hawaii's "constitution" for sixty years, rewarded the manner in which the Hawaiians had yielded up their sovereignty. It granted them full rights of citizenship as Americans.

No longer denied the vote, the natives promptly turned out of office those who had misused them. Sanford Dole was appointed first governor of the Territory by the President in Washington. Other officers were elective, however. Promptly organizing their own political party, the Home Rule Party, the Hawaiians dominated the new Territorial Legislature and sent to Washington as Hawaii's first delegate to Congress that stanch royalist, Robert Wilcox. Later, they made delegate one of their own who could truly represent *all* of Hawaii—Prince Kuhio Kalanianaole. He was regularly returned to office by them until his death twenty years afterward, and saw to his people's welfare as a young queen who had never ruled over them might have done.

David Kawananakoa, the other princely "cousin" who had shared Kaiulani's life (and who, it was generally assumed, would have become her husband), lived on in the Islands until his death in 1908. He eventually married the beautiful Abigail Campbell, who by strange coincidence had been born in the very room and in the very bed as had Kaiulani herself. Abigail's father had purchased the Emma Street mansion when Archibald Cleghorn moved his family to Ainahau. His bride later confided to a close friend that "of course I never could have married David if Kaiulani had lived."

The other young man who had been so attentive to her—her father's personal choice, Andrew Adams—remained in Hawaii through decades in which his devotion to Kaiulani's memory became a popular legend. Stories were told of his bringing flowers to her tomb even as an old, old man.

In 1908 a distinguished literary visitor to the Islands, Ella Wheeler Wilcox, was so touched by Kaiulani's story that she added her own lei of verse to the legend:

> Dreaming of thrones, she grew from child to maid,
> While under Royal Palms soft fountains played.
> She saw herself, in Time's appointed hour,
> Ruling her kingdom by love's potent power;
> Her radiant youth, imperially arrayed.
>
> Where tropic suns were tempered by sweet shades,
> Protecting love her pleasant pathway laid;
> And there she dwelt, a Princess in her bower,
> Dreaming of thrones.
>
> Marauding changes brutally invade
> Her Island home; and yet Time's hand is stayed
> Her name has left the fragrance of a flower.
>
> She sleeps in beauteous youth that cannot fade,
> Dreaming of thrones.

When his duties as United States minister ended, Harold Sewall returned to Maine. On December 2, 1899, the Sewall shipyards at Bath launched the three-masted steel bark *Kaiulani,* built for a San Francisco company and intended for the California-Hawaii trade.

Towed from Bath to New York and then sailed around Cape Horn, the *Kaiulani* kept her Princess's name plying the Pacific until she was sold in 1907 to the Alaska Packers' Association. Much later, when steam had replaced sail altogether, she was not scrapped as were her sister barks. Instead, she was chartered to a succession of Hollywood film producers for use in pictures set in sailing days. Although she was differently furbished for each such appearance, the *Kaiulani* became the American public's chief image of how a square-rigged windjammer had looked.

Bitter to her last day against the men who had usurped her power, Queen Liliuokalani shut herself away in the Dominis mansion until her death in 1917. A full eight years after Kaiulani's passing, Charmian London (visiting Honolulu with her author husband Jack) said of the fallen Queen that "the narrow black eyes . . . gave the impression of being implacably savage in their cold hatred of everything American. . . . I offered her a dubious paw, which she touched gingerly, as if she would much prefer to slap it." Not until America entered World War I did the Stars and Stripes fly from the staff at Washington Place. Had the Hawaiians been offered only this less gentle royal example of adjustment, their assimilation as Americans might have been delayed for many a decade.

But of all those who personally remembered Kaiulani, it was natural that her father's memories should be most poignant. Archibald Scott Cleghorn lived on at Ainahau, surrounded by his gardens and by mementos of his royal daughter and wife, until he died in October 1910. Those final years—inevitably, years of loneliness in a house once filled with gaiety—were dedicated to civic and charitable duties. Shortly before his death, he revealed a long-cherished plan.

"Kaiulani is dead and gone," he said, "and there are not many more days left to me. I want to leave some lasting memorial to the memory of Kaiulani and I do not know anything more appropriate than to dedicate this beautiful home of hers to the people of Hawaii as a public park. Kaiulani's mother and I worked for years to beautify it and it has been Kaiulani's home all her life . . . and her life was ended here."

In accordance with this last tender hope, the old man in his will directed his trustees to offer his premises at Ainahau to the government, with the proviso that they be forever kept a public tropical park named Kaiulani Park, and closed to visitors (who might damage the botanical specimens) from sunset to sunrise.

A near riot broke out in the Territorial Legislature over Cleghorn's bequest. Various interests stirred up opposition to its acceptance, crying that appropriations for such a park's upkeep would be excessive and that the restrictions placed upon its use were "unfulfillable" and "insulting." Although the chief spokesman against the park was a legislator of colorful political reputation called "Too Bad" Jack Kalakiela, it was understood that at the core of the opposition stood heirs through Kaiulani's half-sisters who had hopes of inheritance. After several stormy sessions, the offer was rejected.

Thus left unprotected, the acres of Ainahau passed through a variety of fortunes until—no longer a vista of rare beauty, no longer a loved private retreat—they were cleared for the construction of the tallest (and in many respects, the most handsome) of the many new hotels that a growing tourist boom brought to Waikiki. The Princess Kaiulani Hotel is surrounded with handsome tropical groves which in some measure bring back the peacock gardens of old.

Well before Cleghorn's death, a Honolulu public school was named in Kaiulani's honor; and her father presented to it the pastel portrait of her painted in London and showing her in her yellow ball gown with a nosegay of marguerites. A slip from the great banyan at Ainahau was planted in the school yard and continues to grow there, decades after the destruction of the parent tree. Kaiulani School still observes the birthday of its Princess with appropriate annual exercises.

On September 21, 1921, the *Advertiser* carried a pathetic little story:

> Royal relics . . . are at a low ebb of public interest, judging by the low price received at public auction yesterday morning for the quaint little phaeton which the late Princess Kaiulani formerly drove around Honolulu. . . . In its day it was . . . an equipage

which attracted attention whenever the pretty little Hawaiian Princess made her drives in public. Yesterday it was brought down to Colonel Will E. Fisher's auction rooms. . . .

The persuasive voice of the Colonel, however, fell upon unheeding ears. . . . He asked for $100, then $50, then $25 . . . and a Portuguese finally bid $5. Somebody bid $5.50, and the Portuguese bid $6 and it was knocked down to him.

Noting the trend of a new era, the story added, "It is a bad day for vehicles propelled by anything but a gasoline motor."

Yet Kaiulani's direct impress upon Hawaii's fortunes endured beyond the dawn of the automobile age and well into the time of the airplane.

On December 7, 1941, a cloud of sea-based Japanese war planes came roaring in over the Islands, making Pearl Harbor an eternal name and plunging the United States of America into its Second World War.

Had a young schoolgirl in 1894 not written to her dethroned aunt, politely declining the suggestion that she marry a Prince of Japan and thus save her country from American annexation, a weak provisional government could not have prevented the alliance. On that December day forty-seven years later, Hawaii almost certainly would then have been a Japanese military base. The bombs that ripped Pearl Harbor could have hit California or Oregon or Washington instead. And if that had happened, it is unlikely that a fiftieth American state would have been created of her Islands six decades after "Hawaii's Hope," the Princess Kaiulani, had set aside forever her "dreaming of thrones."

Suggested Reading

Index

Suggested Reading

The difficulty in recommending additional reading to those who may wish to know more about Princess Kaiulani is simply stated. No such printed material exists.

The details of her life presented in this book have been assembled from sources beyond the reach of the average reader—from private diaries, from personal interviews with those still living who remember her, from old letters (many of them written in Hawaiian), from materials in the Archives of Hawaii and libraries and museums in Honolulu, from individuals in Hawaii and in England, from the files of various newspapers of the period, from unpublished manuscripts. Until now, these have not been readily available except as scattered scraps.

However, Kaiulani's life story was also the story of her people at a vital hour in their history. There are several books which may add to the reader's knowledge of the little kingdom she was trained to rule and the events of which she was a part. Among these, we suggest:

Craft, Mable. *Hawaii Nei.* New York: Godfrey Weiners, 1899. An unbiased picture of Hawaii during the last summer of its independence.

Damon, Ethel. *Sanford Ballard Dole and His Hawaii.* Palo Alto, Calif.: Pacific Books, 1957. A biography of the man whom Kaiulani's enemies chose to lead them, presenting the public events of her life from his viewpoint.

Fergusson, Erna. *Our Hawaii.* New York: Knopf, 1942 (out of print, but available in many libraries). A book containing chapter-long vignettes of several historic Hawaiian personalities, including Kaiulani.

Field, Isobel. *This Life I've Loved*. New York: Longmans, 1940. Twelve chapters of this autobiography by Robert Louis Stevenson's stepdaughter describe her life in the Honolulu of King Kalakaua and give a colorful and personal picture of the world of Kaiulani's childhood.

Liliuokalani. *Hawaii's Story by Hawaii's Queen*. Boston: Lothrop, Lee and Shepard, 1898. The Queen's own account of her overthrow.

Mellen, Kathleen Dickenson. *An Island Kingdom Passes*. New York: Hastings House, 1958. By far the most complete account of the death of Hawaii's monarchy, much of it drawn from previously unavailable sources and interpreted by a writer with a special understanding of the Hawaiian people.

Stevenson, Robert Louis. *Collected Letters*. Edited by Sidney Colvin and appearing in various editions. Many of the letters were written from Honolulu during his stay there and offer interesting sidelights on his visit, always so tenderly remembered by Kaiulani.

To this brief list it may be forgivable if we add a general history of Hawaii of our own, *The Hawaiian Islands from Monarchy to Democracy* (New York: Viking Press, 1956) in the belief that it will provide a background for the events of Kaiulani's time.

Index